To Audrey and Ralph

Best Wishes

From

Guy

Xmas 2019

MISSING – DIED – SURVIVED
THE SENIOR BROTHERS AND THE GREAT WAR

First published 2019

Copyright © Guy Senior 2019

The right of Guy Senior to be identified as the author of this work has been asserted in accordance with the Copyright, Designs & Patents Act 1988.

Sources other than the author's are acknowledged, and reproduced with permission.

Digital restoration of author's black and white photographs by 'Image Centre' of Bath (www.imagecentre.com).

British Library Cataloguing-in-Publication Data. A catalogue record for this book is available from the British Library.

Published under licence by Brown Dog Books and The Self-Publishing Partnership, 7 Green Park Station, Bath BA1 1JB

www.selfpublishingpartnership.co.uk

ISBN printed book: 978-1-83952-073-0

Cover design by Kevin Rylands
Internal design by Andrew Easton

Printed and bound by CPI Group (UK) Ltd, Croydon CR0 4YY

This book is printed on FSC certified paper

MISSING – DIED – SURVIVED
THE SENIOR BROTHERS AND THE GREAT WAR

Guy Senior

CONTENTS

LIST OF ILLUSTRATIONS

List of Abbreviations

AM	Air Mechanic
BEF	British Expeditionary Force
Bn	Battalion
&c	*et cetera* (and the rest)
Capt	Captain
CCS	Casualty Clearing Station
CO	Commanding Officer
Coy	Company
Cpl	Corporal
CWGC	Commonwealth War Graves Commission
DAG	Deputy Adjutant-General
DCM	Distinguished Conduct Medal
do	*ditto* (the same)
F/Sgt	Flight Sergeant
GOC	General Officer Commanding
GRU	Grave Registration Unit
HA	Hostile Aircraft
HAA	Hostile Anti-Aircraft (artillery)
HE	High-Explosive
IWM	Imperial War Museum
Jasta	*Jagdstaffel* (German fighter squadron)
Kofl 4	*Kommandeur der Flieger 4* (German Air Commander report of its 4 Army – on the Ypres sector)
KOYLI	King's Own Yorkshire Light Infantry
L/Cpl	Lance Corporal
Lt	Lieutenant

LVG	*Luftverkehrsgesellschaft* (German aircraft manufacturer – abbreviation used in British air combat reports to indicate a certain type of enemy aircraft)
MC	Military Cross
MG	Machine Gun
NCO	Non-Commissioned Officer
POW	Prisoner of War
Pte	Private
RAF	Royal Air Force
RE	Royal Engineers
RFC	Royal Flying Corps
TF	Territorial Force
VHF	Very High Frequency
VTC	Volunteer Training Corps
WGS	Wakefield Grammar School

INTRODUCTION

I found the letters after my father died. There were six of them in total, tucked away in the drawer of a long-neglected wardrobe. No ordinary letters, they had been written to my great-grandfather to console him on the loss of his gallant son, killed whilst serving on the Western Front. The first of the letters described the circumstances of this young officer's death, followed by an assurance that the writer would visit during his next period of home leave to offer whatever further condolence he was able. No ordinary letters and no ordinary man. On the one hundredth anniversary of his death, I visited my great-uncle's grave in France and paid my respects to this man with whom I shared a surname, a man I knew only by reputation. That November I attended the Remembrance Day service at the school he had attended as a pupil. As the last post echoed, I trained my eyes on the school war memorial and focussed my thoughts on two names in particular – there could quite easily have been a third. And if there had been, this book would never have been written.

Wakefield Grammar School War Memorial

Chapter One
God's Choicest Blessings

Arthur Senior was born on 5 March 1863 in Batley, Yorkshire. His father was a woollen spinner by the name of Joshua, and his mother's name was Maria (née Farrar). Maria seems to have been illiterate because her 'signature' on Arthur's birth certificate is simply a cross, next to which is written 'the mark of Maria Senior' in handwriting which matches that of the registrar, a Mr Henry Brearley. Arthur had a Methodist upbringing and regularly played the chapel organ during services. He also had a particular gift for mathematics, something which he put to good use in his chosen profession of accountancy. On 28 May 1891, he married Mary Ann (affectionately known as 'Polly') and together they had three sons named Joseph, Walter and George. Joseph was the eldest boy and was born on 22 May 1892. His birth was followed two years later by that of Walter on 21 February 1894, with George being born a further year later on 15 September 1895. Walter was the only son officially to be given a middle name – Talbot – which was his mother's maiden name. The birth certificates of Joseph and Walter reveal that they were both born at 2 Belgrave Terrace in Stanley, a sub-district of Wakefield. Curiously George's birth certificate records him as having been born at 2 Pinderfields in Stanley. Nevertheless, he was almost certainly also born at 2 Belgrave Terrace (Pinderfields being the general name of the area), and it seems likely that the registrar made an error of omission when filling in his entry in the birth register. Below is an early family photograph. Polly is on the left, sitting with George on her knee. Joseph is standing in the middle and Walter is sitting on a footstool in front of him. To the right of the photograph is Arthur, sitting with hands clasped and sporting a moustache typical of the era.

Arthur and Polly Senior with Joseph, Walter and George (Gent family collection)

Tragically, Polly died on 26 May 1901 at the age of 35. Her death certificate reveals that she had been injured when she fell off her bicycle. She then contracted tetanus, presumably through a cut or graze sustained in the accident, and died 16 days later through heart failure.[1] Joseph, the eldest of her boys, had celebrated his ninth birthday just four days previously. Walter was aged seven and George just five. The effect their mother's death had on the boys can only be guessed, but it seems likely that Joseph, being the eldest, would have now taken on a more responsible role in the family, keeping a watchful eye on his younger brothers and perhaps also comforting his father in his bereavement.

Arthur remarried on 28 December 1904 in Boston, Lincolnshire. His new bride was Mrs Kate Hallam née Grundy, also a widow, whose first husband (Percy Hallam) had died in March 1902. Kate had a daughter from her previous

---

1 According to her death certificate, Polly died at 1 Belgrave Terrace. This is also the home address given in the school register when Joseph first attended Wakefield Grammar School.

marriage named Bessie, who now became stepsister to Joseph, Walter and George. Bessie is pictured below. There are surviving letters, written to her during the war, which are quoted in later chapters.[2]

Bessie Hallam (Author's collection)

JOSEPH

All three brothers were educated at Wakefield Grammar School. Joseph joined the school in September 1903, aged 11, on a Storie Scholarship which covered all his school fees. He shone academically, Latin being one of the subjects at which he excelled, and won his form prize in every year. Also a keen sportsman, he played both cricket and rugby for the school. He appears in the First XV team photograph for the 1909-10 rugby season with his younger brother Walter. In this photograph, shown below, Joseph is sitting cross-legged second from the left on the front row. Walter is standing in an open collar on the far right of the back row. Also pictured are two of Joseph's close friends: Guy Richmond Aspinwall, who is seated to the left of Joseph; and Robert Stanley Dixon, who is standing in the middle of the back row and wearing a school uniform rather than a rugby kit.

---

2 Arthur and Kate later had three more children together named Frank, Mary and Margaret – born in 1905, 1909 and 1911, respectively.

Wakefield Grammar School First XV 1909-10

(Image © Wakefield Grammar School Foundation Archives)

Joseph left Wakefield Grammar School in July 1911 and in the Oxford Senior Examination he was ranked first out of 14,000 candidates nationally. His exam success secured him a place at the University of Cambridge, but before the start of term he embarked upon a sightseeing tour of France. During the course of this summer trip, he sent several postcards to friends and family back in England. The first of these postcards was sent to his father and postmarked 14 August 1911. On the back Joseph writes the following message: 'Arrived safely at Chartres this morning. Travelling all night on steamer & train. Just going to look at cathedral. Joseph.'

Joseph's postcard from Chartres Cathedral (Author's collection)

Another postcard, franked with the same date, was sent to school friend Guy Richmond Aspinwall. This card, offering a different view of Chartres Cathedral, reads as follows: 'Arrived this morning. Glorious cathedral. Frightfully hot. Senior.' There are three other surviving postcards which were sent back to Joseph's family in Wakefield, and they depict the cathedrals at Reims and Chartres and also a Romanesque church at Vézelay. In addition, there are 17 unmarked postcards, mainly depictions of cathedrals and churches, which Joseph brought back as mementos of his trip. By studying all these postcards, both marked and unmarked, the following itinerary can be pieced together: Chartres, Paris, Cravant, Vézelay, Auxerre, Soissons, Reims, Laon, Amiens, Rouen. Below is a particularly fine postcard bought in Paris, showing a seemingly bored gargoyle peering down from Notre-Dame.

Joseph's postcard from Notre-Dame (Author's collection)

Joseph's French trip occurred during a period of social unrest in Britain which is sometimes referred to as 'The Great Unrest'. This period, in the years leading up to the outbreak of the Great War, saw a wave of strikes throughout the country involving miners, railwaymen and dockers. The disruption caused by one such strike is referred to by Joseph in a postcard he writes at Auxerre, date-stamped 19 August 1911: 'Am beginning to wonder whether I shall be able to get home.

Strike seems to be serious.' A few days later, Joseph sends a card from Reims, in which he writes: 'Am glad to see in the papers that the strike has ended. Some chance of getting home Wednesday or Thursday.'

Following his return to England, Joseph received a postcard from school friend Stanley Dixon – to thank him for the card he had sent whilst in France. Stanley writes the following: 'Many thanks for PC. You seem to have been having a good time in France with Mr & Mrs B. You say that you visited several cathedrals – Are you by any chance thinking of taking up Architecture? I hope so. You would find it jolly interesting. RSD.'

Clare College Cambridge group photograph, taken in 1914. Joseph is standing in the middle row, third student from the left (Author's collection)

In the autumn, Joseph went up to Clare College at the University of Cambridge. Here he studied Classics on an Open Classical Scholarship, Cave Exhibition, West Riding County Major Scholarship and School Leaving Exhibition. The following spring he received another postcard from Stanley, date-stamped

31 May 1912, which read as follows: 'Thanks for P.C. I suppose you will be commencing your exams soon. Best wishes for your success. I have just returned from Whitsun holidays which have lasted almost a week. Are you playing cricket? Stanley.'

Joseph passed all his first-year exams and was placed first in his college, as a result of which his scholarship was increased and extended for a further two years. He graduated in the summer of 1914, taking the Classical Tripos with first-class honours. He was also a recipient of the Owst Prize, which was founded by Anthony Owst-Atkinson in 1869. This prize was awarded to Clare students of Classics placed amongst the first six in the university examinations. In addition to this, Joseph won Dr Greene's Cup for General Learning, made from sterling silver, which displayed the following Latin inscription:

Josepho Senior, A.B.
Ex dono Roberti Greene A.M. Tamworthiensis
Collegii de Clare olim Socius
ut alumnos ejusdem collegii
ad litterarium ac scientiae studia
diligenter exsequenda
Impelleret
Anno Domini MCMXV.

Translation
To Joseph Senior, BA
Gift of Robert Greene, MA, of Tamworth, former Fellow of Clare College, to encourage the alumni of the same college to the study of literature and science. AD 1915.[3]

(Robert Greene lived from circa 1678 to 1730 and was educated at Clare College. He was awarded a fellowship by the college in 1703 and devoted much of his life to the defence of the Christian religion. In his will, he left instructions for the formation of a 'Greene Benefaction', which was the body responsible for

---

3 This translation has been kindly provided by Dr Rupert Thompson (University of Cambridge Classics Department).

awarding this cup to Joseph. A Greene Cup for General Learning is still awarded annually to undergraduates of Clare College to this day.)

Doctor Greene's Cup for General Learning, awarded to Joseph in 1915 (Author's collection)

WALTER

By the time Walter arrived at Wakefield Grammar School, the family address had changed from Belgrave Terrace to 'Normandale' on Bradford Road in

Outwood. Walter first attended the school in September 1906, aged 12, on a Storie Scholarship. He excelled academically and displayed a particular aptitude for Mathematics and German – the latter subject being one he may well have needed to call upon in later life. He also played rugby for the First XV and appears in the team photograph reproduced earlier in this chapter.

Walter left school in 1910 and then began an apprenticeship as a woollen merchant, working under an Alfred Talbot, who appears to have been his maternal uncle. Woollen manufacture was a major industry in Wakefield at this time and surviving

Walter as a boy

evidence suggests that Walter acted as a commercial traveller, work which would have involved taking samples to prospective buyers.

GEORGE

George arrived at Wakefield Grammar School in September 1907, aged 12, on a Foundation Scholarship which covered half his fees. Although less academically gifted than his brothers, he was still a bright pupil and won his form prize in 1909 and 1910. He was also a very capable rugby player. Several years after leaving school, he asked his old headmaster, Mr Matthew Henry Peacock, for a reference. Mr Peacock had the following to say about his former pupil: '[George] obtained a high reputation both for work in the Class Room and for efficiency in School Sports: his character was excellent.' Below is a form photograph from July 1909, which shows George seated in the second row, third boy from the left. Three boys sit between him and the bearded Mr Peacock, whose mortar board singles him out as the most senior of the three masters pictured.

Wakefield Grammar School form photograph 1909 (Image © Wakefield Grammar School Foundation Archives)

George left Wakefield Grammar School in July 1911 and in 1912 entered the University of Leeds as an agricultural student on a two-year course which covered Agricultural Chemistry, Veterinary Science and Book-keeping. He gained work experience for this course by living on Wood Farm, North Lees, Ripon – possibly working for a Mr W.T. Stephenson.

Arthur wrote a letter to George on 4 April 1913. This letter was written on 'County Hall' headed notepaper, as he was working in the West Riding Treasurer's Department in Wakefield at the time. Arthur's letter is laden with biblical references and full of sound fatherly advice. It also includes a touching reference to first wife Polly:

My dear Boy,

You are entering upon another chapter in your life – let this one be better than the last – you have opportunities – make the best of your chances. Keep your eyes before you. I hope that you will find your new home a good and happy one. Begin as you hope to continue. <u>Be regular</u> and <u>punctual</u>. <u>Rise early</u> and <u>keep a cheerful heart</u> – <u>"whatever thy hand findeth to do, do it with thy might."</u> Never forget your earthly Father believes in you, loves you, & hopes & expects you to be a gentleman at all times wherever the path of duty leads you. Let your mind sometimes dwell upon the memory of your Mother's goodness – simple in life, pure in word & thought. Her sainted life has been a help & blessing to me, and I have no doubt that her spirit constantly hovers over her dear boys.

<u>Behold thy Mother "keep thy heart pure – for out of it are the issues of life"</u>. Read good books, whenever you have time – make time to read your bible regularly. I shall be very glad to hear that you have joined some church. Take an interest in any good movement if you have opportunity. But be most careful in the friendships you form.

That God's choicest blessings may be showered upon you is the prayer of your affectionate Father.[4]

---

4 This letter was found amongst George's effects without its original envelope. It seems likely that it was written to him whilst he was staying at a new address near the University of Leeds.

Chapter Two
Some shooting
for a blind man

On 28 June 1914 Archduke Franz Ferdinand of Austria was assassinated in Sarajevo, capital of the recently annexed province of Bosnia. The assassin was Gavrilo Princip, a Bosnian man who was acting on behalf of a group of Serbians violently opposed to Austrian expansion in the area. In retaliation for the killing, Austria issued an ultimatum to Serbia and, when it failed to meet its stringent demands, used this as justification for declaring war on the country. Although this was Austria's war, Germany was bound by its alliance with Austria-Hungary to support it, and this led Germany into conflict with Russia – a country which had already vowed to protect Serbia, and also a country which had an alliance with France. Germany thus declared war on Russia and, fearful of French mobilisation, also declared war on her ally France. Great Britain was also allied to France through the *entente cordiale* agreement of 1904, but was initially reluctant to become involved. Germany's implementation of the 'Schlieffen Plan' would, however, prove pivotal in forcing Britain's hand.

On 4 August 1914 German troops marched towards France via neutral Belgium, a route designed to avoid the strong line of fortresses along the French/German border. This tactic had originally been devised by Count Alfred von Schlieffen and was intended to bring about a swift and decisive victory against the French by encircling her troops and attacking them from the rear. However, in implementing this plan, Germany had underestimated Britain's resolve to honour the 1839 Treaty of London – a commitment to protect Belgium's neutrality. Britain promptly declared war on Germany, taking her place alongside her French and Russian allies in what would initially be referred to as 'The European War'.

Britain had no compulsory military service when the war began and was reliant on a small but highly trained army of regular soldiers, backed up by an equally small number of Territorial Army reservists. Conscription would eventually come into force in 1916, but in the years prior to this the British Expeditionary Force had its numbers bolstered by volunteers. These men came from all social classes and professions and were united in their shared sense of moral duty to protect Belgium and, by so doing, uphold the honour of the British Empire. Volunteers stepped forward in their hundreds of thousands, many anxious not to be late for a conflict which would be over by Christmas – or so it was thought. Joseph, Walter and George were three of the many who voluntarily gave up the comforts of their home life in order to pit themselves against unknown dangers overseas.

George in KOYLI Regiment uniform, the collar and cap badge displaying the regimental motif of a French horn encircling the White Rose of York (Author's collection)

Despite being the youngest, George was the first of his brothers to serve on the Western Front. He enlisted with the Territorial Force, aged 19 years old, and swore his oath at York on 9 November 1914. Initially serving as a private in the 1/1st Yorkshire Hussars, he was assigned to 'A' Squadron and given the service number 2792. Upon joining, his medical inspection report described his vision as being 'normal with glasses' and his physical development as being 'good'.[5] George was

---

5 The primary source material used in this chapter for George's medical and military history comes from TNA WO 374/61329.

deployed overseas on 17 April 1915 and his unit first saw action at the Second Battle of Ypres, which took place from 22 April until 25 May 1915. Ypres was located to the west of Belgium and its retention was seen by the British as being of the utmost importance, both strategically and symbolically – the violation of Belgium being the catalyst for Britain's involvement in the war. The Second Battle of Ypres saw the controversial use of chlorine gas by the Germans. This deadly gas was used to devastating effect against the British, French and Canadians.

Joseph in West Yorkshire Regiment uniform, the collar and cap badge displaying the regimental motif of a galloping horse (Author's collection)

George survived his first year in the Army unscathed, although there is a record of him suffering from enteritis for a period of two days at the end of August 1915. The following year, on 9 August 1916, he returned to England and from 5 September he undertook officer training at the No.6 Officer Cadet Battalion in Oxford. On 19 December 1916, having successfully completed his course of instruction, he was appointed to a commission as a second lieutenant in the 2/4th Battalion of the King's Own Yorkshire Light Infantry – commonly abbreviated to KOYLI. Promotion to this particular regiment would have been a source of great pride to George as the 4th Battalion's headquarters were in his home town of Wakefield. The Grammar School also had strong links to this battalion, and as a boy George may well have seen these volunteer soldiers performing drills on the school's games field, something they were permitted to do with the full blessing of the governors.

In the summer of 1914, Joseph had successfully completed his degree course at the University of Cambridge and was now setting his sights upon a career in the higher branch of the Indian Civil Service. With this end in mind, he had enrolled upon a special course at Wren's College in London and taken up residence at 80 Cambridge Gardens. However, after just six weeks there, he altered his plans and volunteered for military service instead. Unlike George, Joseph applied to join as an officer and submitted his application in August 1914. His application was eventually accepted in October, when he was offered a commission in the 11th Battalion West Yorkshire Regiment. There is a surviving Army physical fitness report, compiled at Cambridge on 16 November 1914, which accurately reports his age as being 22 and describes his hearing, teeth and vision as being 'good'.[6]

Joseph posing with other officers of the West Yorkshire Regiment at Aldershot

Above is an undated photograph which was taken at Aldershot, presumably following successful completion of officer training. Joseph is standing on the right,

---

6 The primary source material used in this chapter for Joseph's medical and military history comes from TNA WO 339/1739.

his right arm tucked behind his back and his left gloved hand pressing down on a swagger stick. His rank of second lieutenant is evident from the single pip that appears on his uniform jacket sleeve – two pips denoted a lieutenant, and three pips a captain, as displayed by the officers sitting, respectively, right and centre.

Whilst at Aldershot, Joseph wrote a letter to his stepsister Bessie. This letter provides the earliest glimpse of his days in the Army. In this letter, Joseph's classical education is hinted at from his use of Roman numerals to indicate the month of December:

Oudenarde Barracks
North Camp
Aldershot
30. XII. 14

Dear Bessie

Please thank Father & Mother for their letters to hand this morning, also George for his, if he is at home. Tell Father I got the Burberry all safe yesterday afternoon; all parcels seem to have been very much delayed this Christmas. I wonder if George got my second letter. We are moving away from here tomorrow into billets at Crowthorne, where my address will be as before c/o Mrs Brougham, Brougham House, Crowthorne, Berks.

We stay there for about 7 days & then return to barracks, & from there go into billets again, but not at Crowthorne. I don't know what our address will be there. Nearly 30 of my men failed to turn up in time after their Xmas Leave, & 5 of them are still missing, all married men.

The weather here is dreadful, nothing but wind & rain, & the fields are in flood all over.

Hope all are well. Best love to all.

Joseph

In the above letter, Joseph makes reference to a number of his men failing to turn up on time after their Christmas leave. Joseph's men are pictured below, in a photograph taken at Bramshott Camp in Hampshire. Second Lieutenant Senior is seated on the fourth chair from the right.

Joseph with his men at Bramshott Camp in Hampshire (Author's collection)

In March 1915, Joseph wrote another letter to Bessie. This letter is quite remarkable as it makes direct reference to Lord Kitchener, who was Asquith's Minister of War and famously appeared in numerous recruitment posters pointing a finger at all who met his inescapable gaze:

27 Earls' Avenue
Folkestone
4 March 1915

Dear Bessie,

I am sending you one of our Regimental brooches, which I got in Folkestone the other night: hope you will like it. We arrived here all safe last Monday feeling very fit. The weather was remarkably good the whole time & my face is quite red now with the sun. Most of the men stuck it very well indeed: we covered 117 miles in the 7 days & had comparatively few men falling out. One day we did 25 miles or more, Dorking to Edenbridge, but got into the latter place almost at our last gasp. My feet were rather weary & I developed a small blister, but was really troubled very little on the whole. Kitchener inspected us on the Sunday: we marched past him on the road. I was the first platoon in my company & gave him 'eyes right' with great gusto. He was very pleased with our appearance

& is reported to have said 'The First Army is good, the Second is better, but the Third (ours) licks them all', so we feel quite happy. Folkestone is swarming with French & Belgian people, many of them wounded soldiers, who are convalescing here. Our men are all put up in Boarding Houses, where they have everything provided by the people of the house, beds, food, etc., & as they have been previously accustomed to Army rations only, seem to be living in comparative luxury. We officers, I think, are faring worst of all: we are put into an empty house, which we have to furnish ourselves, if we want furniture, & have to sleep in our camp-beds, which after all are nothing like so comfortable as a spring mattress etc. We were put into private billets each night on the march down from Aldershot & were treated quite well. The experience was a very strange one. Things are a good deal more interesting here than in Aldershot: we frequently have aeroplanes flying over us & torpedo boats are continually passing up & down the channel. All lights throughout the town have to be shaded at night & there is not a gleam showing at all on the sea-front. We go down onto the beach for our parades & find it much more interesting than in Aldershot. Rupert has just had a note from Jack to-night to say that he is probably going out to the front on Sunday or Monday & so Rupert & I shall probably go up to London this week-end to see him. Hope all are well. Love to all.

Joseph

Joseph was deployed to France in August 1915, where he became attached to the 23rd Division Cyclist Corps. The 23rd Division formed part of Kitchener's Third New Army and were initially billeted in Saint-Omer in France, approximately 30 miles west of the front-line town of Armentières. Front-line duties began in September and in October Joseph wrote two letters to his old school friend, Stanley Dixon. Both these letters give great insight into Joseph's earliest wartime experiences. In the first of them, Joseph makes reference to his brother George. He also makes reference to another one of his old school friends, William Harold Armitage, who was a pupil at Wakefield Grammar School from 1904 to 1909. Armitage, or 'Army' as he was sometimes known, was engaged to

Mildred Head. Mildred was the daughter of Charles Head, who was Wakefield Grammar School's Second Master and served at the school from 1887 to 1922. Mr Head was affectionately known as 'Piggy' to his pupils and his daughter therefore became known as 'Milly Piggy':

Envelope addressed to R.S. Dixon Esq., 44 Stanhope Gardens. Queen's Gate, London W. and stamped by censor.

2 October 15

Dear Stanley

Very pleased to get your letter & hear how you have been faring since I last saw you in town: my address has altered & is now

23rd Div. Cyclist Coy
B.E.F.
France

Your letter went to my old Battalion, & then had to be sent on to me here, as a result of which it was some time in transit. As for the long & continued silence, that you talk about, I assure you that I myself am the last person in the world to reproach anyone with anything of the kind because I'm such a bad correspondent: in saying which, of course, I'm protecting myself against future recriminations on your part, but really you never know out here when you are going to have time to write lengthy epistles, or, in fact, epistles of any kind, & so some genius invented the Field Post Card, a specimen of which I sent you the other day. We have been in the fair land of France for 6 weeks now & feel quite hardy veterans. I must say, however, that this military life, even when one is out in the field, leaves me quite cold & is altogether uninspiring. We are billeted in French farm-houses which, as a rule, are particularly obnoxious: the reason is that the French farm-house is invariably built round the farm muck-heap, into which all the filth of the place is emptied. The result, as you can imagine, is a perfect plague of flies accompanied by the most overpowering odour. However, one gets used to such minor discomforts after a while, & the great thing is that we actually have soft beds & linen sheets to sleep in. I must explain that as Cyclists we have nothing to do in our own line as long as the present trench warfare continues, & so our Division has given us the task of running the Divisional Bomb School, in which we instruct the men of the Divisional Infantry in the use of Grenades, Bombs, Trench-Mortars, & such-like. This means that we don't go into the trenches with the Infantry, but stay in our billets about 4 miles behind the firing-line with occasional visits to the trenches to inspect the bomb-stores, etc. My men in their letters home are all exceedingly optimistic about an early conclusion of the war after this last effort of the French, but personally I think we shall have to achieve something much greater before we make any real impression on the Germans. Everything has settled down again in this region after the heavy bombardment of last week & it was heavy, I can assure you; we didn't make any advance with the infantry in this part of the line, & I suppose we shall stay on here the winter over. I've been under shell-fire occasionally & a Taube nearly dropped a bomb on me the other day, but apart from that I haven't seen much warfare, & I don't know that I'm anxious to do so. In normal times the Germans shell certain spots at fixed hours, they stick to their programme in a remarkable way, and the wise man thus avoids those particular spots at those particular hours & he can move about with comparative safety quite close up to the line. W.H. Armitage of Sheffield, engaged to Milly Piggy, is in my Division, & I frequently run across him. My brother, George, who is in the Yorks. Hussars, is quite close to us, and I slip over to see him occasionally: he has been out for about 6 months now & is frightfully fed up with it. I guess I shall be when I have had 3 months, not to mention 6: however, it's far the best plan to be cheerful about things, & we do our best. One thing, that is particularly striking out here, is the fact that the French people continue to live in their houses & go about their work quite close up to the firing-line: in some cases there are people living in their homes not more than 400 yds. from our front-line trench, & they go about their work in the fields quite stolidly altogether regardless of any bullets or shells that may happen to be abroad. Shall be glad to hear from you: letters are very welcome & literature of any kind is

most gratefully received.
    Yours
    Joseph[7]

Soldiers of the West Yorkshire Regiment relaxing between duties, taken from Joseph's
photograph album (Author's collection)

Below is Joseph's second letter to Stanley, written about two and a half weeks later. In this letter, Joseph makes reference to German Zeppelin attacks in England. The first of these took place in January 1915, when civilians in Great Yarmouth and King's Lynn were bombed from the air by these hydrogen-filled airships:

---

7 This letter was originally published in *Some Other and Wider Destiny: Wakefield Grammar School Foundation and the Great War*, by Elaine Merckx & Neal Rigby (Solihull: Helion & Company, 2017). It is one of four letters written to Stanley which are reproduced in this book. Permission to reprint them has been kindly granted by Stanley's grandson, Philip Dixon.

Envelope addressed to R.S. Dixon Esq., 44 Stanhope Gdns., Queen's Gate, London W. and stamped by censor.

19 Oct 15

Dear Stanley

Very many thanks for the book, which arrived the other afternoon. We eagerly devour all literature that comes our way because on our part of the line things have been for the most part extremely quiet, there is really little else to do but sit on our haunches & read when we have once performed our absolutely essential duties. The weather is now becoming wintry & we are all donning thick underclothing etc. I wish the [dash here in original] war was over, don't you? Write & tell me about the last Zeppelin affair: don't fear the Censor.

Yrs.

Joseph

Excuse short note: am in haste to catch post, will write more later on.

Walter in West Yorkshire Regiment uniform, the collar badge displaying the regimental motif of a galloping horse (Author's collection)

Walter was the last of his brothers to enlist and he joined at Wakefield on 16 October 1915, aged 21. According to a letter written by his father several years later, he had just completed his period of apprenticeship in the woollen manufacture industry and obtained a very good position as a manager. This may account for the delay in him volunteering – almost a year after his brothers had done so. It is known that Walter was a member of the Volunteer Training Corps prior to enlistment and this may shed further light on the matter. The VTC was formed shortly after the outbreak of war in order to provide military training for those who were unable to enlist, but who wanted to contribute to defensive duties at home. Some of these volunteers joined because they were too old for enlistment, whilst others had business or family commitments which made it difficult for them to do so. Walter would clearly have fallen into this latter category, and it is also possible that his father wanted him to stay at home for his own financial security. Whatever the true reasons might have been, it seems the pull of the Army eventually proved too great. With Joseph and George already serving overseas, it was perhaps only a matter of time before Walter would feel compelled to join them. After all, how could *he* stay at home whilst both his brothers were risking their lives abroad? The numerous recruitment posters urging onlookers to 'remember Belgium' would certainly have raised this question in Walter's mind, even if others hadn't vocalised it.

Upon enlistment, Walter was given the service number 8843 and began his Army life as a private in the 29th (Reserve) Battalion Royal Fusiliers. By January 1916 he was in Oxford, where he was undertaking officer training for a commission in the 3/6 Battalion West Yorkshire Regiment. In common with his younger brother George, Walter wore spectacles. There is a surviving medical certificate from Oxford, dated 19 January 1916, which records that he was myopic: the vision in his right eye is recorded as being 6/24 (equating to a modern prescription of – 175) and the vision in his weaker left eye is recorded as being 6/36 (equating to a modern prescription of – 225).[8] Although Walter could see perfectly well with glasses, his 'blindness' is referred to in a letter that Joseph sent to him later that same month. Joseph

---

8 The primary source material used in this chapter for Walter's medical and military history comes from
   TNA WO 374/61338.

wrote this letter from France, where he had been serving with the Cyclist Corps for the past five months. In his letter, Joseph makes reference to 'the Hun' – slang for a German:

23/1/16

My dear Walter

You appear to have been doing 'some' shooting for a 'blind' man: I hope you'll never make worse practice against the Hun, if ever you come up against him. I think your V.T.C. work must have stood you in great stead, also the Institute shooting-gallery, what? You are in rather a peculiar position at present, due to come out here on a draft, & expecting to have your commission gazetted before long. If the C.O. of the Battalion has nominated you & sent in all your papers to the War Office, & you are gazetted in due course, you will simply have to return to England to join your regiment with perhaps a few weeks' experience at the front. Supposing you do come out here before your commission matures, I strongly advise you to make the most of your opportunity & get to know as much as you can about things: with that to back you up you should be a person of some standing in your battalion, & I can see all sorts of things happening. So far as I can remember, the kit that I have got at home consists of the following:-

       Camp Bed with blankets

       Wash Basin & Bath (canvas) with frame

       Waterbottle & Haversack

       Manoeuvre Bag

You will want in addition Flea Bag (Sleeping Bag): the Jaeger Brand is best, & don't forget when sleeping on a camp-bed, that you want blankets underneath to keep the cold out as much as on top: I learnt that in the hard school of experience. By the way, the folding-frame of my camp-bed needs repairing, & I should ask them to get it done in Wakefield at once. You will also need a Wolseley Valise, a thing like a hold-all, in which you roll up blankets, flea-bag, clothes, etc., & sleep in at night wrapped up in flea-bag & blankets. That will complete camp-kit. As for uniforms I advise two outfits ie, two tunics of whip-cord, & two pairs of breeches, strongest Bedford cord or the criss-cross fabric (I forget its name) [up arrow here in original to indicate later insertion by Joseph when he remembers the name of the fabric] ^ got it, Barathea. Really good boots are the only ones worth getting, & they want breaking in. Long Field Boots are undoubtedly the things for the trenches, & I should buy some straight away, if I were starting now. Don't get a Burberry or Great-Coat: a Thresher & Glenny Trench-Coat is the only thing suitable on active service: It combines the water-proof & British Warm, & is cut short so that the bottom doesn't get caked with mud, as is the case with the ordinary Burberry. The long water proof is really no protection for the knees & legs, because the wet always works up. In the way of equipment you will want Sam Browne belt, revolver (which get through the quarter-master), field-glasses (prismatic), compass (get the Magnapole compass; the prismatic variety is not necessary for the Infantry Officer), map-case (get a good sort: the cheap ones don't last), electric torch (Orilux is best, in fact the only one: don't be put off with any other, even though it does cost a guinea). That is about all that is really necessary: Of course, there are all sorts of luxuries, which you can get, if you have the cash & the inclination. By the way, I have forgotten to include a British Warm: get one from Buckle. Weather improving here slightly. No news from George since his return. Rupert's birthday last Wednesday: he was out of the trenches in rest billets & we celebrated the occasion together. Next week we are having for instruction in bombs some men from a division newly out from England, & are making elaborate preparations for putting the wind up them. Keep me posted in the progress of events.

J.

The above letter contains another reference to Rupert, whom Joseph had previously mentioned in his letter to Bessie on 4 March 1915. This was a cousin, also serving with the West Yorkshire Regiment: Rupert Kershaw Talbot was the son of Edwin (Polly's brother) and was born on 19 January 1892. Joseph's letter helps to pinpoint Rupert's identity by indicating that his birthday was 'last Wednesday'. This positive identification helps, in turn, with the identification 'Jack', who is also mentioned in Bessie's letter. This was Rupert's brother, John Wilkin Talbot, who had been a mine engineer before the war and served with the Royal Engineers in a tunnelling company.

This advertisement for military waterproofs appeared in a copy of 'The Sphere' magazine in October 1914

Walter was posted to the 7th Officer Cadet Battalion on 7 April 1916 and then appears to have spent some time at Curragh Camp in Kildare, Ireland. On 23 June he was granted a commission as second lieutenant with the 6th Battalion (The Prince of Wales's Own) West Yorkshire Regiment. His commission document has survived to the present day and is reproduced below:

George by the Grace of God, of the United Kingdom of Great Britain and Ireland and of the British Dominions beyond the Seas,

King, Defender of the Faith, Emperor of India, &c.

To Our Trusty and well beloved <u>Walter Talbot Senior</u> Greeting:

We, reposing especial Trust and Confidence in your Loyalty, Courage, and good Conduct, do by these Presents Constitute and Appoint you to be an Officer in Our Territorial Force from the <u>Twenty-third</u> day of <u>June 1916</u>. You are therefore carefully and diligently to discharge your Duty as such in the Rank of <u>Second Lieutenant</u> or in such higher Rank as We may from time to time hereafter be pleased to promote or appoint you to, of which a notification will be made in the London Gazette, and you are at all times to exercise and well discipline in Arms both the inferior Officers and Men serving under you and use your best endeavours to keep them in good Order and Discipline. And We do hereby Command them to Obey you as their superior Officer and you to observe and follow such Orders and Directions as from time to time you shall receive from Us, or any your superior Officer, according to the Rules and Discipline of War, in pursuance of the Trust hereby reposed in you.

Given at Our Court at Saint James's the <u>Twenty-fourth</u> day of <u>June 1916</u> in the <u>Seventh</u> Year of Our Reign.

<u>Walter Talbot Senior</u>   By His Majesty's Command
   <u>Second Lieutenant</u>
     Territorial Force

Walter's commission document was signed on 24 June 1916. By way of coincidence, 24 June was also day one of the seven-day artillery bombardment that preceded the Battle of the Somme.

Chapter Three
Down on the Somme

On 1 July 1916, British and French troops launched a combined assault on the German lines in Picardy, Northern France. Their aim was to wear down the German Army and relieve pressure on the French fighting at Verdun. The British Army focussed its efforts on a 15-mile battlefront between Serre in the north to Montauban in the south, whilst the French attacked to the south on both sides of the River Somme. Thirteen British divisions and six French divisions were committed to this operation and the battle lasted for 141 days, before grinding to a halt on 18 November.

On 31 July – one month into the offensive – Joseph wrote a letter to his old school friend, Stanley Dixon. Joseph's former division, the 23rd, were involved in the fighting and had been successful in wrestling Contalmaison from the Germans – one of the few early successes enjoyed by the British. The 23rd Division had entered the battle on 3 July, when they relieved survivors of the 34th Division. On 10 July, after several days' fierce fighting, the 11th West Yorkshire Regiment managed to secure Bailiff Wood; and it was from here that the 8th and 9th Yorkshire Regiments launched a successful attack on the village of Contalmaison. The 23rd Division were relieved by the 1st Division on 11 July, having suffered almost 3,500 casualties. In his letter, transcribed below, Joseph refers to the casualties of his battalion (11th West Yorkshire) as those 'outed either temporarily or the other thing':

Envelope addressed to R.S. Dixon Esq., c/o Miss Hayward, Wilbury Road, Letchworth, Herts and stamped by censor.

IV Corps Cyclist Bn.
B.E.F.
31/7/16

Dear Stanley

With us it's almost a case of '(Infantry) men may come & (Infantry) men may go, But we go on for ever.' We've taken a step up, & are now Corps troops instead of Divisional troops as you'll see by the address, the consequence is that we're left in our old stagnation, whilst our late comrades have been doing things down on the Somme. We were taken away from the 23rd about a couple of months ago now & together with the Cyclist Companies of two other Divisions (one Regular & one Territorial) were formed into a Battalion under the IV Corps. We're feeling very sick about it just now, because when you've gone through the terrific grind of training in England & have done nearly 12 months with the same people out in France it's rather a wrench to be left behind when they go away to attempt something more inspiring than the dismal routine of trench warfare, which on our part of the line goes on to all appearances just as if there were no 'big push' happening away South of us. So here we are with whole skins as yet. The 23rd did magnificently & captured Contalmaison, but like everybody who was in the show, had to pay the penalty. About ¾ s of the officers & I don't know how many of the men of my battalion were outed either temporarily or the other thing & I was very disheartened about it for a time, but I've become philosophic about it now & decided that there's nothing to be gained by troubling over such things. Army, of course, was killed when they were still up here with us: I've located his grave & I told Piggie all that I knew about it; you will probably have heard. As you say, we can't realize that we shan't see again this side of the border line such good fellows as he, Chris Sugden & Billy Appleyard. I used to see Army frequently out here & we always had long chats together about old times &

laughed over the comic incidents of the days when we were raw schoolboys. He had proved himself a very capable officer, & it was a hard blow to the 9th Yorks. when they lost him. Of course, it was the filthiest of luck that he should get pipped at all, because they were in reserve billets a mile & a half behind the line, & it's the last thing that you expect there. We are at present engaged on a digging-job under the R.E.s & live under canvas in a wood about 1½ miles behind the line. We sally forth each night about 9 p.m., march up to the trenches, wrestle valiantly during the hours of darkness with a very hard and reluctant earth, then crawl home with the dawn to breakfast and bed. The open-air life is quite pleasant chiefly because the weather has been behaving very well, & brother Boche so far hasn't worried us at all – (I'm touching wood alright). When we've finished this work, I don't know what's going to happen to us. Perhaps another big biff & the Deutschmen will be scooting hard for the Vaterland with us mounted on bikes in pursuit. Who knows? I don't think. Leave, of course, has been stopped for a couple of months & there's no telling when it will open again, but I'll certainly look you up at 36 Bloomsbury when next it falls to my happy lot to be in Blighty. Don't let too long an interval elapse before you give me tidings of yourself again, & if I'm not a model correspondent you must make allowances for a brain now dulled by this war's monotony & a consequently unready pen: it's a fact. Give my best respects to your people.

    Yrs. Ever

    J.

In the above letter, Joseph refers to the deaths of three fellow ex-pupils of Wakefield Grammar School: Chris Sugden (Second Lieutenant Christopher Babington Sugden) was killed on 25 May 1915 in the Bois-Grenier Sector whilst serving with the 4th KOYLI. He was the first old boy of Wakefield Grammar School to die in the Great War and was a pupil at WGS from 1904 to 1912; Billy Appleyard (Lieutenant William Appleyard) was killed on 22 August 1915 in the Dardanelles, whilst serving with the 6th Battalion Yorkshire Regiment. He was a pupil at WGS from 1905 to 1912 and then studied at Clare College,

Cambridge – the same college as Joseph; 'Army' (Lieutenant William Harold Armitage) was killed on 22 May 1916, whilst serving with the 9th Battalion Yorkshire Regiment. He was killed before the start of the Battle of the Somme, whilst his battalion was 'still up here with us'. This provides a clue as to where Joseph is writing from, since soldiers tended to be buried near to where they fell. The Commonwealth War Graves Commission records that Lieutenant Armitage is buried at Tranchée de Mecknes Cemetery, Aix-Noulette – approximately 10 miles north of Arras, to the west of Lens.[9]

'(Infantry) men may come & (Infantry) men may go, But we go on for ever' is a (partial) quotation from 'How the brook reaches the river' by Alfred, Lord Tennyson (1809-1892). Joseph's familiarity with this poem, and by implication Stanley's, too, suggests that both boys had studied (and memorised) it whilst pupils at Wakefield Grammar School. The capitalisation of the letter 'b' would tend to suggest that it had been memorised quite literally. The opening lines are reproduced below, and it is quite possible to imagine Joseph quietly reciting these lines to himself as he went about 'the dismal routine of trench warfare':

I come from haunts of coot and hern,
I make a sudden sally
And sparkle out among the fern,
To bicker down a valley.
By thirty hills I hurry down,
Or slip between the ridges,
By twenty thorps, a little town,
And half a hundred bridges.
Till last by Philip's farm I flow
To join the brimming river,
For men may come and men may go,
But I go on for ever.

Joseph in a trench (Author's collection)

---

9 The full obituaries of all WGS alumni who died in the war can be found in 'Some Other and Wider Destiny'.

BESSIE'S BIRTHDAY

On 20 August 1916, Joseph wrote a letter to his stepsister Bessie to wish her a happy birthday. Bessie was born on 24 August 1898 and, at the time of writing, was four days away from her eighteenth birthday. Joseph's uncertainty about her precise age may be genuine, but it seems more likely that he is teasing when he suggests a much lower age for her:

20th August 16

My dear Bessie Herewith my felicitations & best wishes for many happy returns of the day. I really forget how much it is this time: isn't it either 13 or 14? Let me know; I should like to be certain about the precise number. It's very sad that although they cater for practically every other taste that soldiers are heir to, the Expeditionary Force Canteens don't provide for birthday presents, unless a tin of salmon, an ounce of Navy Cut or a card of Bachelor's Buttons is considered suitable. I don't myself & so will you buy yourself something with the enclosed note? If I could only get to a civilised spot, I should make a purchase myself & so save you the trouble, but it can't be done.

Is George still at home? I haven't been told yet whether he's merely on leave or whether his papers have gone through & he's now going to have a spell in England: I imagine it must be the latter, because so far as I know all ordinary leave is stopped. It will be a very welcome change for him; 18 months' continuous sojourn in this land is quite sufficient for one time.

I heard from Walter the other day & I'm hoping very much that we shall be able to meet some-where, when he's sent up from the Base to join his Regiment.

We are still in the same spot engaged on the same work as of old, & I haven't got any news.

My best love to all.

Yrs affectionately
Joseph

Joseph mentions both his brothers in his letter to Bessie. At the time of writing, George was back in England about to commence officer training in Oxford and Walter was in France, heading towards the Thiepval sector of the Somme.

'Navy Cut' was a brand of tobacco popular during the war, as illustrated by this magazine advertisement from October 1914

WALTER'S LETTER

The day after Joseph wrote his letter to Bessie, Walter also wrote to wish her a happy birthday. To the author's knowledge, this is the only letter written by Walter which has survived to the present day. In it, Walter describes his journey to the battlefront:

Envelope marked 'on active service' and addressed to Miss B.F. Hallam, c/o Mr A Trigg, The Gables, Canwick, Lincoln England; Black postmarked '22 AU 16 – FIELD POST OFFICE 168'; Red hexagonal stamp marked '[PAS]SED FIELD CENSOR 198.'

Monday 21/16

My dear Bessie,

I am hoping that this will reach you in time for me to wish you many happy returns.

After spending a week down at the base camp I have now moved up the line & am waiting a few miles behind the line to join my battalion. We were under canvas at the base camp & were quite close to the sea in fact we could see it from the tents but unfortunately we were too busy during the day to bathe. We were only allowed 3 hrs off every day 6-9pm, & there was nothing really to do except get out of camp for a little time. We had quite a good crossing it was very fresh & rolled quite a lot but I enjoyed it very much.

I have moved right down to the south of our line & am at present in a small village, five of us are billeted in a dirty little farm-house & yesterday evening did a great culinary effort: I've bought some peas & potatoes & boiled the former & fried the latter & with some bread butter, bully & 'vin rouge' had a most excellent repast & we were ready for it. We set off at 3 o'clock on Saturday afternoon & arrived at our destination at 4.30 pm Sunday & then had 5 hrs walk. We did not know that we were to be so long in the train & so had not provided ourselves very liberally. However with a good breakfast of bacon & some eggs we bought from a farm house we are now feeling very enriched.

It is a jolly fine morning & we have aeroplanes continually going over & occasional rumblings of guns, just enough to remind one what we are here for.

I expect to be in the midst of it in a few days.

My address is

> 6th West Yorkshire Regt
> B.E.F.
> France.

Give my love to Aunt Fil & Uncle & seeing that it is your birthday, a kiss for yourself,

Walter

At the start of this letter, Walter refers to an unnamed base camp where he had been staying for the past week. Its location, within view of the sea, suggests that it was near to a French port. From here Walter refers to moving 'up the line'. This is purely a figure of speech and gives no indication of the direction he actually travelled. Similarly, the length of the train journey (just over 25 hours) gives no real indication of the distance travelled, since troop trains were notoriously slow.[10] Walter's address is equally vague: '6th West Yorkshire Regt B.E.F. France'. At the time of writing, this address would have revealed nothing to the reader. However, today, with the benefit of a published history of the battalion (Captain E.V. Tempest DSO MC, *History of the Sixth Battalion West Yorkshire Regiment: Volume 1-1/6th Battalion*, Bradford: Percy Lund, Humphries & Co, 1921), it is possible to fill in some extra details:

At the time Walter wrote his letter, the 6th West Yorkshire Regiment was at Léalvillers, which was approximately nine miles west of Thiepval. Given that this was his destination, it can be deduced that his train journey came to an end at Amiens. Furthermore, Walter indicates that he is waiting to join his battalion, which would tend to suggest that he hadn't quite reached Léalvillers yet. It therefore seems likely that he is writing from somewhere between Amiens and Léalvillers. In truth, the location of his 'dirty little farm-house' can only be guessed, but it is just possible that Walter stayed in Varennes. This village had previously been used by the 6th Battalion and was notorious for being one of the dirtiest villages in which the battalion ever stayed – although it should be noted that Joseph had a similarly unpleasant experience when he was billeted in a French farmhouse further to the north of the country, as recounted in his letter to Stanley Dixon on 2 October 1915.

One of the final details of Walter's letter is his description of buying bacon and eggs from a local farmhouse. In his history of the battalion, Captain Tempest has the following to say about the locals of the Somme region: 'The men...

---

10 Robert Graves, the famous poet and author, served as an officer with the Royal Welch Fusiliers, which had its base camp near Le Havre. In his memoirs, Graves describes a long train journey from Le Havre to Béthune, where he disembarked before marching his platoon a further 10 kilometres to join his battalion at Cambrin village: 'The troop-train consisted of forty-seven coaches, and took twenty-four hours to arrive at Béthune, the railhead, via Saint-Omer. We detrained at about 9 p.m., hungry, cold, and dirty.' Robert Graves, *Goodbye to All That* (London: Penguin Books, 1960; first published by Jonathan Cape, 1929), pp. 95-96.

found that "le franc Picard" was a good type of Frenchman, who did his best to make them comfortable without charging outrageously for it'.[11]

THIEPVAL

Walter had not been with the 6th Battalion when the Battle of the Somme had begun on 1 July. By the time he did join them, his battalion had already been involved in a number of skirmishes in the Thiepval sector and suffered many casualties as a result. Approximate casualties for the first two days of engagement had been 14 officers and 250 other ranks. Here at Thiepval, as elsewhere along the battle line, the enemy's strength had been underestimated and German machine-gun fire had proved devastating. Critically, the British artillery bombardment which preceded the initial attacks had failed to impact upon the opposing dugouts, many of which were built deep underground and strongly constructed. The result was that the advancing infantry had been cut down by German soldiers who had re-emerged relatively unscathed from their reinforced defensive positions.

We know from Walter's letter that he joined his battalion around 21 August. At this time the 6th Battalion was undertaking training in preparation for an attack planned for 3 September. As part of this training, attacks were mounted on taped trenches used to represent the German lines the men would be facing. On 26 August, the 6th Battalion moved from Léalvillers to Hédauville, where they relieved the 2nd Battalion Royal Irish Rifles in the South Bluff, Authuille; and on 2 September, they moved to assembly trenches in Aveluy Wood in preparation for the 'big push' the following day.

THE BATTLE PLAN FOR 3 SEPTEMBER

The plan was to attack the Saint-Pierre-Divion trenches along the Thiepval ridge, with the objective of capturing and consolidating the enemy front and support lines. This attack was to be undertaken by the 39th and 49th Divisions. The 49th (West Riding) Division was to utilise two brigades, which would be the 146 Brigade on the left and the 147 Brigade on the right. 146 Brigade had at their disposal the 6th and 8th Battalions of the West Yorkshire Regiment and were given instructions to attack with the 6th Battalion on the right and the 8th

---

11 Tempest, 'History of the Sixth Battalion', p.72.

Battalion on the left. Specialist bombing parties (carrying Mills grenades) were attached to both these battalions and they were to move up with the second line. Both the first and second lines of the attack were to consist of one and a half companies of men from each of the battalions.

The specific objective of Walter's battalion was to capture a German trench system called 'The Triangle' – between points 67, 16 and 09 on their special operation maps. To the immediate right of Walter's battalion, the 5th Battalion Duke of Wellington's Regiment (part of 147 Brigade) had the difficult task of capturing 'The Pope's Nose', a dominating salient in the enemy line. The following map indicates the location of 'The Triangle' and the relative positions of the 6th and 8th West Yorkshire Regiment Battalions. Each of these battalions had an attacking frontage of 250 yards:

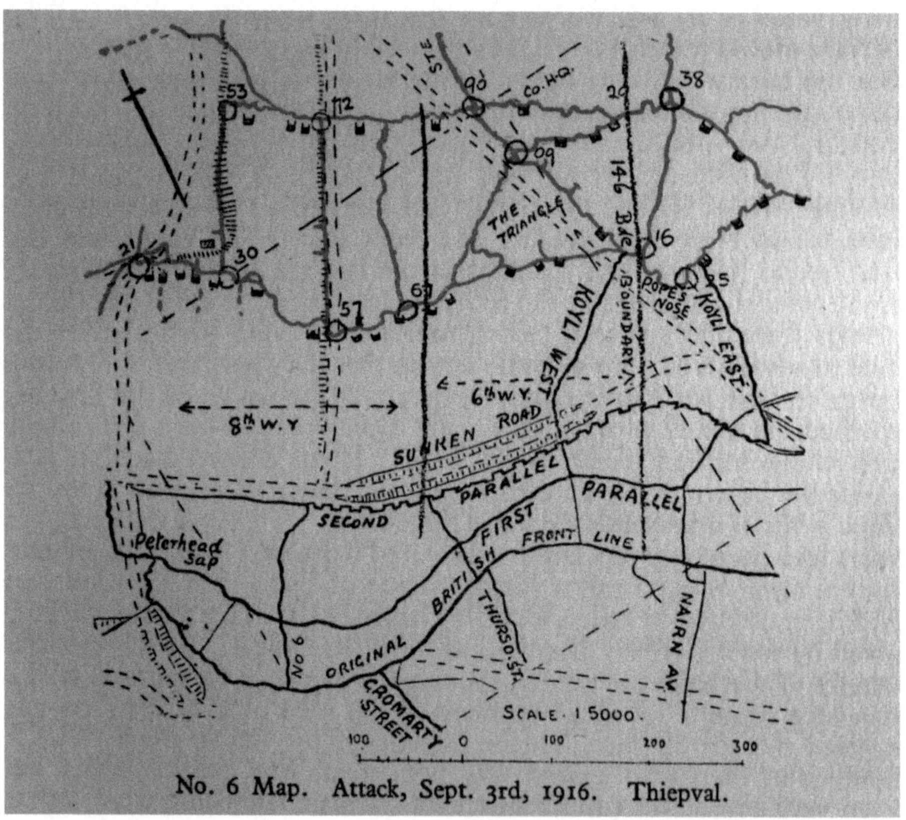

No. 6 Map. Attack, Sept. 3rd, 1916. Thiepval.

This map is reproduced from Tempest, 'History of the Sixth Battalion', p.117

THE BATTLEFIELD

The attack was to be launched from the section of the British line which ran along the northern edge of Thiepval Wood. The original front line here had been about 400 yards from the enemy. However, following the failure of the initial attack on 1 July, two new trenches had been carefully dug in front of this line to reduce the distance to about 200 yards. These two new trenches were named the first and second parallels and, as their names suggest, ran parallel to the original front line. The second parallel was the closest to the enemy and stopped just short of 'The Sunken Road', a notorious spot in no man's land which had been the scene of many British casualties on the first day of the Somme Offensive. For the September attack, soldiers were expected to cross no man's land and reach the German front line in three minutes. Ladders were placed in the parallel lines to help facilitate this and get the men quickly out and over the top. The front line attackers had orders to take the enemy front line, whilst the second line had orders to pass on through the enemy front line and take the enemy support line.

THE DAY OF THE ATTACK

On Sunday 3 September at 1:30 a.m., Walter left Aveluy Wood with the other men of his battalion and crossed the river Ancre by the South Causeway. He assembled in the second parallel with the other members of 'D' Company shortly before dawn. A few minutes before 'zero' (5:10 a.m.), the whole of the front line quietly climbed the ladders before them and lay out on the open ground. Behind them, the second line moved up from the first parallel to occupy the trenches which they had just vacated. And then, at exactly 5:10 a.m. the British artillery barrage began. As the barrage crept forward, Walter rose to his feet and, with the other members of 'D' Company, advanced steadily across 'The Sunken Road' and on into no man's land…

There were approximately 350 men of the 6th Battalion West Yorkshire Regiment who went 'over the top' on 3 September. Out of this number, 33 were killed, 175 were wounded, and 33 were declared 'missing in action'. Walter fell into the latter category. Later that same month Joseph wrote the following letter to Stanley Dixon:

Envelope addressed to R.S. Dixon Esq., Wayside, Wilbury Road, Letchworth, Herts and stamped by censor.

26th Sept. 16

My dear Stanley

Yes, unfortunately the 2/Lt W.T. Senior, whom you saw reported in the official lists as missing, is my brother Walter & as yet we have had no definite information as to whether he has been made prisoner. His regiment, the tenth W. Yorkshires, was in the attack somewhere about Thiepval on Sunday September 3rd, their job was to take the Boche front line, & hold onto it, when taken. They got across alright, but my brother was wounded on the way & was taken down into a German dug-out to be dressed. The Boches then counter-attacked & our fellows had to go back leaving many wounded and prisoners, as you would see from the list of Officers reported Missing. We are hoping daily to get tidings from him in Germany, & all we can do is to wait patiently I suppose. There seems to be very good grounds for hoping that he is prisoner in German hands, & if so, we shall get some communication from him in due course.

I am very sorry to hear that your brother has been so badly hit, & do hope that he will pull round alright.

The casualties we are suffering seem to be terrific to us, who are only accustomed to an army of a few hundred thousand, & we haven't yet realised that we have now become a big Military as well as a Naval Power engaged in a desperate fight to a finish, but I really believe things are now beginning to go the right way. The Boches and their friends are now on the defensive on every part of the front & we are making magnificent progress. I shouldn't be in the least surprised, if the line goes snap down on the Somme before many weeks are passed, if only the fine weather that we are getting just now continues. We are very much nearer to achieving it than most people imagine: whether we can bring that necessary extra pressure to bear the next month or so will show. The Corps General told us the other day that the Boche is very desperate now,

& has been driven back in places right behind his organised system of trenches, & is merely clinging on to such hastily dug defences as our artillery will allow him to prepare.

We are still out of the fighting radius: of course, we are making things as lively as possible for Mr. Boche by means of bombardments and raids, but all the activity is entirely on our side, & we aren't yet attempting anything serious. Whether we shall do so, time will show.

I applied to be transferred to the Flying Corps about a month ago & have to go to be interviewed next Saturday morning. I hope I shall manage to get in because I think the work must be very interesting & in it I fancy I see an escape from the dull monotony that I've complained of so much in my letters to you. I feel I can't stand another winter's idleness with the Cyclists.

Have you ever heard of or come across an architect called Dale in London? We have him in my company: he is an extremely clever fellow & therefore it goes without saying rather a comic cyclist platoon commander. I believe his forte is country houses.

If you've been visiting Cambridge lately I hope you've been duly impressed: next time you go, call in at Clare, & ask for 'fat Hall' of the Rabbit Warren, who was my gyp. Give him a pourboire & he'll tell you very interesting stories.

Do you know that Aspinwall is up in Town doing medicine at Guy's? He was slightly wounded at the beginning of the year and the Authorities then sent him back to his bones.

Hope you are keeping fit. My best respects to your people.
Yrs. Ever
J.S.

In the following months, Arthur Senior received several first-hand accounts of what had happened to Walter:

9/14/1531.
Dear Mr Senior,

I received your letter dated 25th September today. It has been redirected from my home address.

I am glad you have written because I shall be able to give you details of what happened up to the time of the German Counter Attack but unfortunately I am not able to state what finally happened to your son.

No doubt you know that he was in D. Company and in the first line of the attack on the morning of the 3rd September.

We got across "No Man's Land" all right and started to work in the German front line trench your son with D. Company was operating on my right. We were not in touch with them so we tried to bomb along in their direction. I got so far along when I came to one of the numerous dugouts at the door of which was stood a German. He fired at us with a rifle so I threw a bomb at him and he then ran down the stairs of the dugout. I threw a second bomb which burst in the opening of the dugout and this apparently scared them, because immediately a German rushed up from the dugout and said "English Officer down stairs". I had the German covered and went to the dugout called down and to my great surprise it was your son who came up. I asked him what had happened and he told me that he had been taken prisoner and put down into this dugout. After this he joined our bombing party and did good work. We bombed along some distance and then got information that the Germans were preparing for a counter attack and therefore we decided to collect our forces together. There were three Officers and a few men left. The Officers were Mitchell Senior and myself. We decided to wait for the counter attack and then to take our chance back through "No Man's Land". We were not long waiting for the counter-attack within a few minutes they were on us and got within 15 yards before we made a dash. At that time we were all quite close together. I got back all right but I believe Mitchell and your son were both caught by the wire and probably had to "hands up" and go back to the German Trenches. I did not see them after we left the trench. It is impossible for me to say exactly what did happen to him but I hope he is a Prisoner of War. I know how very anxious you must be, the dreadful uncertainty of the affair is so trying for you and Mrs Senior. If there is anything else I can do please let me know.

Yours Sincerely,

(Signed) Stanley G. Hearn.

British Red Cross & Order of St. Joh[n]

10th October, 1916

Lieut. W. Talbot Senior, 6th West Yorks.

Pte. Oliver 864, D.Co. 6th West Yorks, states:-

I saw him with 2nd Lt. Turner in the German trench. Mr Turner was wounded in the hand. When we got the order to retire I saw that the Germans had hold of him. Both were left in the trench when we came away. This was at Thiepval on Sept. 3rd.

British Red Cross & Order of St. John.

16th October, 1916.

Lieut. W.T. Senior, 6th West Yorks.

We have received a report from L/Cpl. Bottomley, 3123, 6th West Yorks. D.Co. now in the 3rd Southern General Hospital, Masonic Hall, Oxford, whose home address is 19, Grafton Street, Manchester Road, Bradford. He states:-

"On Sept. 3rd in front of Thiepval an attack was made about 11.30 a.m. The attack was not a success and we had to come back to our original line. I was told the next day by L/Cpl. Sharp 6. D.XIII that Lt. Senior and Lt. Turner were last seen fighting in the first German line. They had rushed on ahead in front of their men and were taken prisoners. L/Cpl. Sharp told me that the two officers made a good fight for it. They killed some Germans and tried to escape but were caught again. Everyone was talking about it at the time and saying that they were prisoners."

British Red Cross & Order of St. John.

3rd November, 1916.

Lieut. W. Talbot. Senior, 6th West Yorks.

We have yet another report which seems to corroborate what we have already sent to you. It is given us by L/Cpl. H.Bruce, 1303 last week in hospital in France, who says:-

"It was between Thiepval and the Ancre on Sept. 3rd. The first wave took the first German line. I was with the 2nd wave which went straight over it. But when we got about 40 yards beyond it we had to fall back. Mr Senior was in the 1st German line and was being rushed into a dug-out by some Germans. Cpl. Pearce and 8 men ran to get him out but were surrounded by about 40 Germans. This is the last we know about them. We had to retire to our own lines and can only say that if alive they are prisoners. An enquiry has been held about him."

---

338 Moorside Road,
Ecclesfield,
Bradford.
7/11/16.

Dear Sir,

In reply to your letter received this morning, I will give you all the news I can regarding your son.

On September 3rd we went over to capture some trenches, this was about 5.10 in the morning, we got right across to the enemy's lines and your son jumped right into the enemy's trenches, he was got hold of by three of the Germans and put into one of their dugouts, we had to return back to our own lines and he was not there and we came to the conclusion that he was prisoner, but I should have thought by now you would have heard from him. I do not think myself that he is dead without he put up a fight and tried to get away, and in that case he may have got killed or wounded, and if in the latter case he may not be in a position to write. I sincerely hope that you will hear better news before long, he was well liked in our platoon and in the company and we were all very sorry to lose him. For all he had not been in the trenches before, he went over the parapet like a man who had been there before. As regards myself I was not seriously wounded and I am now on my ten days sick leave.

Yours truly,
(signed) Joseph Webster.
(L/Cpl.)

Dear Sir,

As my son 2nd Lieut. C.H. Mitchell was with your son in all the attack of the 3rd September, I thought you would like to know that Captain Hearn cam[e] to see us yesterday. He wrote to you recently, I believe, and also to us but it was a great pleasure to us to see him and hear his account of what took place.

The 3 were amongst those selected to lead the attack at daybreak, and well they justified the choice. The worst feature was that distant German guns enfiladed both trenches, and we lost a lot before the start of the attack. Then the same guns swept the 80 yards of open ground, so that when they took the enemy trench they were isolated. With 6 men they ran to one end to bomb the Germans and then to the other and [sic] to meet another lot. So they went on helping and defending one another, often in tight corners, for an hour and a quarter. Your son greatly distinguished himself and was determined. Towards the end they agreed to try to escape through the barrage when the counter attack came to a head. Just then a large body appeared not 20 yards away. I think they sent the men off first and then made a dash. Hearn got through but nearly stopped a shell. A spectator saw him and also 2 others caught in the wire. These would be Mitchell and Senior. Now the slightest obstacle would keep them long enough and they would have no choice but to surrender. They did well and we must be proud of them. None could do more than they did. They used up all bombs and were using German bombs.

We wrote to Cox & Co., and to the Red Cross.

The Colonel says my son's effects have been sent off.

We are so anxious until we have news. The boys will need clothes and food, and we do not know how they are in health. My wife and I feel it keenly and so must you. Please let us know when you hear anything.

Mrs Turner, wife of Lieut. Turner, lives in Leeds. He is missing also, and another officer, 4 in all.

Yours faithfully,
(signed) Charles Mitchell.[12]

ANALYSIS OF THE ACCOUNTS

There are five first-hand accounts from men who were with Walter on 3 September and one second-hand account from Second Lieutenant Mitchell's father, who relates what he had been told by Captain Hearn following the attack. These accounts are invaluable in piecing together the final moments before Walter went 'missing in action'. Written in response to a request from Arthur, understandably anxious for news of his son, they form a definitive record of all that was known at the time. In total, four officers and six other ranks are referred to in these accounts:

Officers: **Captain Stanley George Hearn** (wounded), **Lieutenant Ernest Arthur Turner** (missing in action), **Second Lieutenant Charles Henry Mitchell** (missing in action), and **Second Lieutenant Walter Talbot Senior** (missing in action).

Other Ranks: **Lance Corporal Bottomley** (wounded), **Lance Corporal Sharp** (alive, unclear whether wounded or not), **Lance Corporal H. Bruce** (wounded), **Lance Corporal Joseph Webster** (wounded, but not seriously), **Corporal Pearce** (missing in action), and **Private Oliver** (wounded).

It is very telling that almost all of the first-hand accounts were written by men who were now lying wounded in hospital, proof in itself that things had not gone according to plan. Lance Corporal Bottomley sums up in a sentence what happened: 'The attack was not a success and we had to come back to our original line.' In his account, Bottomley states that the attack was made about 11:30 a.m. His recollection is, however, at odds with the 'History of the Sixth Battalion', which clearly states that 'zero' was set for 5:10 a.m. and that the attack was already over by 7:00 a.m. Bottomley's error is a timely reminder of

---

12 These six accounts are grouped together in TNA WO 374/61338. They are clearly typed copies of the originals and the final account appears to contain a typing error, i.e. 'they ran to one end to bomb the Germans and then to the other and to meet another lot'. The second 'and' should probably read 'end'.

the fallibility of human memory – it highlights how the recollection of events can differ from one person to another.

The time at which the attack was actually made is accurately recorded by Lance Corporal Webster, who states that it was 'about 5.10 in the morning'. It is clear from Webster's account that he was close to Walter when he went 'over the top', which means that he must have been with him in the second parallel trench. (He may even have been close enough to glance across at Walter's watch in the moments leading up to the 'push'.) Webster has this to say about Walter: 'For all he had not been in the trenches before, he went over the parapet like a man who had been there before'. These are the observations of an experienced soldier, impressed by the determination of the inexperienced officer leading him into battle.[13] Webster reports that they successfully reached the enemy front line, and that Walter jumped right into the enemy's trenches. He was then captured by three Germans and put into one of their dugouts. This account is corroborated by Lance Corporal Bottomley and also by Private Oliver, both of whom make reference to Walter being captured. Both also make reference to Lieutenant Turner, who was seen fighting alongside Walter and was taken prisoner with him.

Lance Corporal H. Bruce was in the second line of the attack, which had orders to pass on over the first German line and attack the support line. Evidently enemy fire forced them to abandon the attack short of their objective: 'When we got about 40 yards beyond [the first German line] we had to fall back'. As Bruce was returning, he saw Walter in the first German line being rushed into a dugout by the enemy: 'Cpl. Pearce and 8 men ran to get him out but were surrounded by about 40 Germans.'

While all this was going on, Captain Hearn was fighting further along in the same front-line trench as Walter, but to the left of him and out of his sight. Hearn reports taking a bombing party and bombing his way along the German trench in the direction of Walter's Company – which must have been somewhere along the line from point 67, heading towards point 16 on the special operation map. Hearn's account of what happened next is quite remarkable: 'I had the German

---

13 There is a record of a Private J. Webster travelling across to France in 'D' Company when the 6th
   Battalion were first deployed on 15 April 1915 (Tempest, 'History of the Sixth Battalion', p.297). If this
   is the same J. Webster, which seems likely, then he had survived active service for well over a year and
   been promoted to lance corporal.

covered and went to the dugout called down and to my great surprise it was your son who came up.' Walter then joined their bombing party and made a good contribution to their efforts. Mitchell's father, relating what he had been told by Hearn, adds the following: 'They used up all bombs and were using German bombs.' Evidently Hearn's bombing party had found these German bombs stockpiled in the German trench and decided to make good use of them. It must therefore be presumed that the soldiers had some prior training in their use, since German bombs were different in design to British ones. Standard issue for the Germans was the *Stielhandgranate* or 'stick grenade'. In order to light the fuse on this device, a cord had to be pulled prior to it being hurled. In contrast, the British were using Mills grenades, which were round in shape and required the removal of a pin.

Hearn relates that the bombing party continued to bomb along some distance until news reached them that the Germans were preparing for a counter-attack. They then collected the remaining men together and made plans to return to the British line. Apart from Hearn, the only other officers left fighting at this point were Walter and Second Lieutenant Mitchell. Mitchell's father relates that there were six men with the officers. These men were sent back across no man's land first to improve their chances of survival, while the officers waited until the last moment to make their dash for freedom. When the enemy got within 15 yards of them, they made a break for it. Between them and the comparative safety of the second parallel lay 200 yards of no man's land, interspersed with coils of barbed wire. Behind them lay the threat of rifle and machine-gun fire.

Hearn has this to say: 'I got back all right but I believe Mitchell and your son were both caught by the wire and probably had to "hands up" and go back to the German Trenches. I did not see them after we left the trench.' Mitchell's father adds the following: 'Hearn got through but nearly stopped a shell. A spectator saw him and also 2 others caught in the wire. These would be Mitchell and Senior.' On first reading of this account, it appears as though Hearn also got caught in the wire. However, if he did, he must have freed himself soon after in order to have returned safely to the British line. The insertion of a comma in the middle sentence renders a more plausible interpretation: 'A spectator saw him, and also 2 others caught in the wire.' But even here there seems to be an element of doubt. By Hearn's own admission, he did not see Walter or Mitchell after they left the German trench. He *believes* that they were caught by the wire, but did not actually witness this happening. It is the unnamed 'spectator' who saw Hearn; and his association with the two other men close by seems to have led Hearn to believe that the two others were Walter and Mitchell – which of course they may well have been, but equally they may not. Once again the uncertainty of human testimony comes into play. Whatever the truth of the matter, this is the final detail we have about Walter – that he was reportedly caught in the wire with Mitchell. Both officers would now be classified as 'missing in action', their final fate a mystery.

WHY THE ATTACK FAILED

The failure of the 6th Battalion to carry out its objectives was replicated by the failure of the other battalions in the attack to do likewise. This failure can be attributed to many causes, not least of all the strength of the German defences. These defences were particularly strong at 'The Pope's Nose' and the inability of the 5th Battalion Duke of Wellington's Regiment to capture this dominating position left the 6th Battalion vulnerable to machine-gun fire enfilading on their right flank. Furthermore, the accuracy of the enemy artillery shelling resulted in much of the second line of the attack being caught in a deadly barrage as it attempted to cross 'The Sunken Road'. The result of all of this was that the second enemy line was never reached and the first enemy line was held too weakly to hold. In the end there was no alternative other than to retreat back to the original line from which the attack had been launched.

THE OTHER OFFICERS

Stanley George Hearn was the ninth child of John and Elizabeth and was born in Dartmouth on 13 March 1888. He was educated at Dartmouth Technical School and later gained employment at the Royal Naval College in Dartmouth as head laboratory assistant. At the beginning of the war he served with the 7th Battalion (Cyclists) Devonshire Regiment as a colour sergeant. He gained his commission on 5 May 1915 when he was appointed second lieutenant with the 6th Battalion West Yorkshire Regiment. He was then promoted to the rank of temporary captain in April 1916.

Captain Hearn's letter to Arthur gives a detailed account of Walter's last-known movements on 3 September. At the start of this letter, Hearn writes: 'I received your letter dated 25th September today. It has been redirected from my home address.' The hospital that Hearn is writing from is not named, but was possibly the 4th London General Hospital in England. Hearn was sent here following 3 September in order to be treated for shell-shock and enteritis. A surviving medical record from this hospital, dated 14 September 1916, records Hearn's home address as being 5 Victoria Terrace in Dartmouth and reports that Hearn 'is troubled with terrifying dreams & feels incapable of any sustained mental or bodily effort'.[14]

Following his stay in London, Hearn received another medical assessment at a military hospital in Exeter. This assessment took place on 20 November and it seems likely that Hearn was sent here due to the hospital's proximity to his home address in Devon. The conclusion of this assessment was that it would be another two months before Hearn would be fit to return to active service.

There is one last surviving medical record, dated 21 December 1916, which was compiled at Clipstone Camp, which is where Hearn had been stationed before being assigned to the West Yorkshire Regiment. The findings of this report into Hearn's state of health are as follows:

> That he was the only officer left when the counter attack was made
> & as he was coming back a shell burst close to him & threw him up.
> He did not lose consciousness. He subsequently shewed symptoms
> of
> (1)   Shell shock
> (2)   Enteritis
> The symptoms of shell shock were as follows – exhaustion &
> wasting – feelings of compression of the head and sleeplessness
> with terrifying dreams. He was incapable of any sustained mental
> or bodily effort for some time afterwards.

The assertion that Hearn was 'the only officer left when the counter attack was made' seems at odds with Hearn's letter to Arthur, in which he relates that there were three officers left at this time. The reason for this discrepancy is unclear, but may simply be due to the doctor paraphrasing what his patient had told him. One thing beyond doubt is the terrible psychological trauma that Hearn suffered

---

14 All medical records in this section are extracted from TNA WO 374/32310.

as a result of his experiences that day.

Second Lieutenant Charles Henry Mitchell (Image © IWM HU 125734)

Charles Henry Mitchell was known as 'The Professor' to the men who served with him. His home address was 148 Chapeltown Road in Leeds and he was the only son of Charles Mitchell, who was a surveyor of taxes. According to Captain Hearn's letter to Arthur, Mitchell was with Walter at the time of the German counter-attack on 3 September: 'There were three Officers and a few men left. The Officers were Mitchell, Senior and myself'. Mitchell's father, relating what Hearn had told him on the day of his visit, adds the following detail: 'I think they sent the men off first and then made a dash.' It is interesting to compare this account with the one that appears in the 'History of the Sixth Battalion':

Lieut Chas. H. Mitchell with about twenty of his men reached the enemy line, and seems to have stayed there longer than anyone else. By about 6-30 a.m. most of his platoon had become casualties, and the enemy were surrounding him on all sides. He told his men one by one to try and get back to our line, but most of them in doing so were killed by enemy rifle fire. In fact only two of his party survived, and reported they were the last to leave him.[15]

This account is curious because it makes no mention of there being two other officers with Mitchell at the time of the counter-attack, i.e. Captain Hearn and Walter. However, the 'History' does contain an earlier reference to a 'Lieutenant Hearne', who was evidently close to Walter during the fighting:

> Lieut. Hearne (A Coy.) reported seeing Lieut. Senior with several men busily bombing German dug-outs.

Although there is a similarity in spelling, there is a difference in rank between Lieutenant Hearne and Captain Hearn; and this would tend to put paid to any theory that this is a typo and the two men are in fact one and the same person. Nevertheless, it is worth pointing out that Hearn was a temporary captain at the time of the attack[16] and so describing him as a lieutenant does not necessarily present a problem. It is therefore entirely possible that 'Hearne' is a misspelling of 'Hearn'. This theory is lent further weight by the following passage, which appears in the same section of the book:

> Lt. Hearne also reported that we had held fairly strongly Point 16, but the enemy counter-attacked and drove us out… Hearne with a few small groups of men remained in the enemy lines till about 6-30 a.m., but by this time the situation was hopeless, and the strong German counter-attack mentioned previously compelled the remnants of the Battalion which still remained in the enemy front line to retire.

Captain Hearn was heading towards point 16 when he freed Walter from the

---

15 Tempest, 'History of the Sixth Battalion', p.119. The following two quotations are also taken from p.119.

16 The Casualty Clearing Station admission book (TNA MH 106/497) records S.G. Hearn's rank as '2 LIEUT', whilst the subsequent medical reports (included in TNA WO 374/32310) record his rank as 'Capt'.

German dugout, and it is quite possible that his party reached this point at the time of the counter-attack. In light of this supporting evidence, it seems a very real possibility that the two men are in fact one and the same, i.e. 'Lieutenant Hearne' was really 'Captain Hearn'. If this theory is correct, then it follows that the author of the 'History of the Sixth Battalion' has combined two different sources without realising that they overlap.

Lieutenant Ernest Arthur Turner (Image © IWM HU 119375)

Ernest Arthur Turner was born in Essex, but took his military oath in Bradford, where he signed up with the Territorial Force on 22 September 1914. His address at the time is recorded as being 19 Ebberston Terrace, Hyde Park, Leeds. He was granted a commission in the Sixth Battalion West Yorkshire Regiment on 10 March 1915, and was twice wounded in action that same year. Both injuries were sustained whilst serving in the Ypres sector, the second incident taking place on 17 December 1915, when he was wounded by heavy artillery shelling prior to a gas attack.

Lieutenant Turner fought alongside Walter on 3 September 1916 and is referred to in the accounts of Private Oliver and Lance Corporal Bottomley.

Mitchell's father also makes reference to him in his letter to Arthur Senior, along with his wife: 'Mrs Turner, wife of Lieut. Turner, lives in Leeds. He is missing also.' Turner's wife was Helen Katharine Mary Turner, née Wilson. She was a teacher at Harvington School in Ealing, where she taught Mathematics and Latin to the young girls in her care. When Miss Wilson had joined this kindergarten school, it had been known as Heidelberg College, a name derived from the birthplace of the woman who had inspired its foundation, a Fräulein Leudesdorf. However, in July 1915 this name was deemed to be no longer appropriate: 'Because of the violation by Germany of the laws of international warfare… the School hitherto known as Heidelberg College shall be called henceforth by a British and not a German name.'[17] Mrs Turner remained at Harvington School whilst her husband was serving overseas. She had married him in April 1915, but he had left almost immediately to serve at the Front. Had the war not intervened, Mrs Turner would almost certainly have resigned her post to become a housewife in Leeds. Instead she remained at the school, waiting for the return of her husband.

---

17 There is a surviving 'next of kin' form which lists Heidelberg College in Ealing (crossed out) as the
address of Turner's wife – from which it has been possible to trace her to Harvington School (TNA WO
374/69849). Additional information on Mrs Turner comes from the centenary booklet of Harvington
School, published by Margaret Franklin in 1990. The quotation is to be found on page 6 of this booklet.

Chapter Four
Flying Corps Matters

'The R.F.C. attracted the adventurous spirits… men who were not happy unless they were taking risks.'[18] These are the words of Cecil Lewis, who served with the Royal Flying Corps during the Great War and later recounted his experiences in his classic book 'Sagittarius Rising'. For Joseph, the attraction was an escape from the dull monotony of trench warfare. Frustrated at not being involved in the recent Somme Offensive, he wanted to take on a more proactive role in the fighting. In his letter to Stanley Dixon, dated 26 September 1916, Joseph relates the following: 'I applied to be transferred to the Flying Corps about a month ago & have to go to be interviewed next Saturday morning.' Depending on the interpretation of 'next Saturday', this interview must have taken place on either 30 September or 7 October. Whichever date it was, the interview went well and Joseph's application was accepted. He was subsequently assigned to Sedgeford-based No.45 Squadron, which was preparing for mobilisation to France – Joseph was to join the squadron once it had arrived.[19]

No.45 Squadron arrived in France in mid-October 1916 and was initially based in Fienvillers, which was to the south-west of Arras and behind the Somme sector of the battlefront. The airmen flew Sopwith two-seater fighter-reconnaissance aircraft, which came to be known by the familiar name of 1½ Strutters due to the distinctive strut arrangement that linked the wings to the

---

18 Cecil Lewis, *Sagittarius Rising* (London: Peter Davies, 1936), p.101.

19 No.45 Squadron had been formed in Gosport on 1 March 1916 and was briefly based at Thetford before moving to Sedgeford. At this time the squadron was still in its infancy and was essentially a flying training school, tasked with preparing its men for operational duty. Whilst in Sedgeford, it also played a nominal role in protecting the country from Zeppelin raids.

fuselage. These aircraft were equipped with Scarff-Dibovsky interrupter gears, which allowed the pilot to fire his forward-facing Vickers machine gun through the propeller blade. The rear Lewis machine gun was mounted on a Scarff ring, which enabled the observer to swivel and elevate his weapon so that it could be fired easily in any direction – from either a crouched or a standing position.

The machines themselves were constructed of wood, wire and fabric and were able to fly at speeds of between 80 and 95 mph, depending on altitude. Once in the air the pilot and observer were exposed to extreme lows of temperature, against which they needed to be wrapped up in several layers of warm clothing in addition to their essential flying caps, gloves and goggles. During patrols, communication with other aircraft was achieved through the use of flares. Communication between pilot and observer was made via rubber speaking tubes, which were threaded through the fuselage and past the fuel tank between the cockpits. The pilot could also maintain visual contact with his observer by means of the small, round mirror that was positioned at the apex of the upper wing support (as illustrated below).

Second Lieutenant Francis Thomas Courtney in front cockpit of Sopwith 7792 (Author's collection)

The above photograph appears in Joseph's photograph album and was taken by him from the rear cockpit of Sopwith 7792, whilst in flight near Sainte-Marie-Cappel. It shows the observer's view of the pilot, in this case Second Lieutenant Courtney. Below is the corresponding photograph, taken by Courtney, of Joseph. A duplicate of this second photograph appears in the Norman Macmillan collection of the Imperial War Museum (reference Q 108678). This duplicate bears the following writing: 'J. Senior February 17'. Despite the implied date, there is reason to believe that it was actually taken on Boxing Day 1916, this being the only recorded incident of Joseph flying with Courtney.[20]

Joseph in rear cockpit of Sopwith 7792 (Author's collection)

Joseph acted as an observer during the whole of his time with No.45 Squadron, although he had aspirations to eventually become a pilot. The observer's role was to make notes on enemy positions and to assist his pilot by keeping a constant lookout for enemy aircraft, using his machine gun to defend or attack where necessary. He

20 A separate copy of this photograph is in the possession of Cross & Cockade International. Their copy has benefitted from the research of the late Jim Brown, and it is through Jim's research that the identity of Courtney as pilot can be confirmed.

was also responsible for exposing photographic plates at key points above hostile territory, strategic reconnaissance being the main thrust of the squadron's work. Once developed, these photographs were used by Army HQ to draw up accurate maps of enemy trenches, artillery positions and troop movements.

NO.45 SQUADRON RECORD BOOK

Joseph joined No.45 Squadron at Fienvillers on 26 October 1916. He was one of five new observers to join that day – two of the others were Maurice Moore and Francis George Truscott, both of whom had previously served with Joseph in the IV Corps Cyclist Battalion. Joseph's first mention in the squadron record book is dated 28 October 1916. The squadron was still not up to full operational strength on this date and the records indicate that there were only seven pilots available to fly and eight available aircraft, four of which were 'unserviceable'.[21] On this day, Joseph embarked upon two practice reconnaissance flights with Second Lieutenant Henry Griffith Pagan Lowe, flying in a Sopwith with the serial number 7788. Both these flights took place in the morning, starting at 9:50 and 11:05, respectively, and the second flight is recorded as being to Arras and back. Lowe was a 28-year-old flying instructor and had been commissioned as a second lieutenant in the Royal Flying Corps on 10 February 1916. The recipient of a Distinguished Conduct Medal, his bravery had been recognised earlier in his career when he had rescued an unconscious pilot from a grounded aircraft shortly before its on-board bombs had exploded. Lowe was the first pilot that Joseph flew with, but these two flights were the only ones that they shared.

On 2 November, Joseph took part in a practice flight and acted as observer to Lieutenant Arthur Willan Keen, who was the Commanding Officer of 'C' Flight at this time. Each squadron was subdivided into three flights of four aircraft each, typically labelled 'A', 'B' and 'C', and Joseph was assigned to the latter. He also appears to have been the first-choice observer for the CO of this particular flight. During their stay at Fienvillers, No.45 Squadron had six men killed in action and several others injured.

On 5 November, No.45 Squadron moved to Boisdinghem, which was to the west of Saint-Omer and in the Ypres sector of the battlefront. Joseph's training

---

21 All squadron record book entries in this chapter are extracted from TNA AIR 1/1787/204/151/3 (01/10/16-31/12/16) and TNA AIR 1/1787/204/151/4 (01/01/17-30/06/17).

continued into this month and on 10 November he undertook target practice with Lieutenant Keen. During this target practice the cartridge guide spring broke on Joseph's machine gun. A similar problem had occurred earlier in the day when Keen was undertaking target practice with Sergeant Taylor, flying in the same aircraft. In Taylor's case the machine gun had jammed. Mechanical faults were a common occurrence at this time and they often had fatal consequences – as demonstrated by the death of Joseph's first pilot, Second Lieutenant Lowe, two days previously on 8 November. Tragically, Lowe had been killed attempting a forced landing after his aircraft engine had failed. His observer, Second Lieutenant Willie Jordan, was also killed in this accident, which occurred during a practice formation flight near Boisdinghem. The funerals of Lowe and Jordan took place on the afternoon of 10 November. Fourteen officers attended the funeral service at Saint-Omer, including Major William Ronald Read, who was the CO of No.45 Squadron.

On 17 and 21 November, Joseph shared two more flights with Keen. The first of these was undertaken as part of a three-aircraft practice formation to Abbeville and Étaples, and the second was as part of a six-aircraft 'reconnaissance' of Dunkirk, Calais and Boulogne. November was also significant as being the first time that Joseph flew with Second Lieutenant Geoffrey Hornblower

Cock. The pair first flew together on 6 November and surviving records indicate that they flew together on 12 further occasions, the vast majority of these being practice flights. Cock was billeted with Joseph and appears in his photograph album. The following undated photograph was taken at Sainte-Marie-Cappel. The lack of foliage in the background suggests that it was taken during the winter, or possibly early spring.

Second Lieutenant Geoffrey Hornblower Cock (Author's collection)

SECOND LIEUTENANT G.H. COCK

Geoffrey Hornblower Cock was born in Shrewsbury on 7 January 1896 and was an architect prior to enlistment. He joined the Artists Rifles Officers Training Corps on 13 December 1915 and, on 3 June 1916, transferred to the Royal Flying Corps as a second lieutenant. He undertook his preliminary aviation training at Christ's Church College in Oxford and was subsequently assigned to No.45 Squadron. Prior to flying out to France, Cock narrowly avoided being disciplined after an incident at the RFC base at Thetford. This incident is worthy of mention here because it gives insight into Cock's character and also illustrates the military regulations of the time.

On Saturday 14 October 1916, Cock had landed at Thetford Aerodrome en route for the Expeditionary Force in France. However, upon landing, he failed to report to the Commanding Officer there – a Major R.G.D. Small. This clearly infuriated Major Small, who later wrote that Cock 'failed to report to me for about 4 hours, and it was only by chance that I was informed of his arrival'. Small continues: 'Later he asked me if he could stay the night in Thetford, and left his address as the Bell Hotel, Thetford. To this I agreed, but impressed upon him that he must be available to leave in his machine the very first moment the weather cleared.'

According to Major Small the weather cleared on Sunday morning, but Cock failed to turn up at the aerodrome. Small then reported him for being absent without leave. Cock eventually showed up on Sunday evening and flew from the aerodrome at 7:00 a.m. the following morning. The seeming pettiness of this incident is compounded by the comedy which later unfurled when Cock's hotel cheque bounced. Mrs Jessop of the Bell Hotel in Thetford returned the dishonoured £4 cheque, informing the military authorities that 'Lieutenant Cock was here two days. He had guests to dinner & luncheon, also had wine. His bill amounts to £4=1=1 for which he paid me 1/11 in cash.' Whether or not Mrs Jessop was ever fully reimbursed for the outstanding amount is unclear, but Cock escaped disciplinary action for being absent without leave 'owing to the necessity of getting pilots and machines over as soon as possible.' It was the Brigadier General of the Training Corps who had the final word on this particular matter.[22]

---

22 Information extracted from TNA WO 339/61967.

SAINTE-MARIE-CAPPEL

On 4 December 1916, No.45 Squadron moved to Sainte-Marie-Cappel (to the east of Saint-Omer), where it was to remain until 16 November 1917. The aerodrome here was pleasantly situated next to a farm with a poplar-lined paddock and the squadron sleeping quarters were Nissen huts, where the men were billeted in pairs. These huts were semicylindrical in shape and had corrugated tin roofs. One such hut features in the background of the following photograph, which depicts Lieutenant Francis George Truscott. The observer's wing badge can be clearly seen here, embroidered above the left breast pocket of Truscott's jacket. Just below this wing badge is a white-purple-white Military Cross ribbon bar – rendered white-grey-white by this black and white photograph. Truscott had been awarded the MC in January 1916 for saving the lives of two other men at Loos (photograph from Joseph's photograph album).

Lieutenant Francis George Truscott (Author's collection)

CAPTAIN W.G.B. WILLIAMS

On 6 December 1916, Captain William George Bransby Williams took over as CO of 'C' Flight, replacing Keen who had been posted back to England on 3 December. From 15 December 1916 up until 26 January 1917, Joseph flew mainly with Captain Williams, and surviving records indicate that the pair flew together on 43 occasions during this time.

Williams was born in Hackney on 6 January 1898 and was 18 when Joseph first flew with him. Williams had been commissioned as a second lieutenant in the RFC on 12 June 1915 and had previously served with No.2 Squadron. He was also the recipient of the Military Cross, awarded in recognition for his work over the Hohenzollern Redoubt during the Battle of Loos. Although clearly underage when he enlisted, he proved himself to be an exceptional pilot. Williams is pictured below, with an affectionate arm around Joseph, in a photograph taken at Sainte-Marie-Cappel sometime between December 1916 and January 1917.

Joseph and Captain William George Bransby Williams (Image © Cross & Cockade International)

Joseph flew twice with Williams on 15 December. In the morning they undertook a test flight in Sopwith A/1083 and in the afternoon they undertook a practice flight in Sopwith 7794, making a total of a five practice landings. It was essential that pilots perfected their landing skills as these early aircraft were quite flimsy and could easily be damaged if not handled correctly. If a pilot misjudged his angle and speed of trajectory, he was likely to cause damage to the machine's undercarriage when he touched down – on what was essentially a grass field. Inevitably such damage did occur, but air mechanics were always on hand to carry out repairs where necessary.

On 16 December, Joseph acted as observer to Williams on a reconnaissance flight with several other aircraft over Aire, Béthune, Armentières and Dixmude. They landed at Abeele and the record book indicates that they flew for a total of two and a half hours. As well as reconnaissance flights, formation practices were also undertaken in this month. On 27 December, the pair flew as part of a three-aircraft formation which followed the following route: Aire, Béthune, Hesdigneul, Bruay, Auchel, Chocques, St.-Venant, Hazebrouck. During December, Joseph was involved in a total of six formation practice flights, the last of which was to Dunkirk. Gun tests also continued in this month and there is another record of Joseph's Lewis gun jamming on the morning of 20 December, although this problem had been fixed by the afternoon.

Joseph's very first aerial photographs were taken on 22 December, with Cock flying as his pilot. This was a practice flight, undertaken in the afternoon, and three photographs were taken of Cassel and the aerodrome. Cassel was an important village to the north of the aerodrome. It served as a useful navigation aid to pilots as it was located on a prominent hill which set it apart from the otherwise flat landscape of the surrounding area. It was also (and still is) home to the *Notre-Dame de la Crypte* church, parts of which date back to the end of the tenth century. Joseph had visited several old churches during his summer vacation to France in 1911 and it is therefore entirely possible that he visited this church, on foot, during his spare time away from the aerodrome.

Joseph flew a total of three times with Cock during December and also flew on one occasion with Lieutenant Francis Thomas Courtney. This is the only recorded incident of Joseph flying with Courtney, and the record book indicates that they were 'testing weather' when they took to the air on Boxing Day 1916. This may well have been a cover for something far more frivolous, i.e. 'going for a joyride'. The cockpit photographs of Joseph and Courtney that feature at the start of this chapter appear to have been taken during this Boxing Day excursion, and souvenir photography may well have been the true objective of their flight that day.

Courtney was, by all accounts, something of a character. Initially flying with No.3 Squadron, he had the distinction of having survived an aerial encounter with German ace Max Immelmann in October 1915. Immelmann's Fokker was one of a new breed of deadly German fighter aircraft and Courtney was fortunate to survive when his machine was badly shot up. After recovering from his injuries, he was assigned to No.20 Squadron and then later to Joseph's squadron. Courtney is pictured below (centre) in a snowy photograph taken at Sainte-Marie-Cappel. The ribbon bar beneath his pilot's wings (barely visible in this photograph) is likely to relate to the *Croix de Guerre* military award he gained prior to joining No.45 Squadron. This photograph is taken from Joseph's photograph album.

Second Lieutenant Allan Stewart Carey (an observer), Lieutenant Francis Thomas Courtney and Second Lieutenant Frank George Garratt (Author's collection)

DEFENSIVE PATROLS

January was a significant month for Joseph, in that it saw his first recorded encounters with hostile aircraft – abbreviated as 'H.A.' in squadron records. The first incident took place on 4 January 1917, whilst on a defensive patrol with Captain Williams in Sopwith A/1075. The log entry for this encounter is quite brief: '1 H.A. seen low down his own side of the line'. The following day, whilst on another defensive patrol with Williams, another enemy aircraft was seen: 'Very cloudy, 1 H.A. crossed the line at NEUVE EGLISE, came as far as BAILLEUL, and then south to ARMENTIER[E]S where he recrossed his own line, persued [sic] him, but did not come within range.' A casual reading of this log entry reveals nothing unusual, but there is a hidden subtext behind the abandoned pursuit: No.45 Squadron did not yet have permission from Wing Command to penetrate enemy lines and had been severely chastised when one of their aircraft had done just that in the previous month, even though this particular penetration had occurred whilst in hot pursuit of an enemy patrol.

On 8 January, two days after his nineteenth birthday, Captain Williams took over as temporary commander of No.45 Squadron, a position he retained until 21 January. Joseph continued to act as his observer during this period, although he intermittently flew with Cock as well. On 9 January Joseph and Cock undertook firing practice: 'Shooting at pond. Vickers working well.' The squadron record book contains many such references to a pond being used for firing practice. The precise location of this pond is not revealed, but it was presumably a safe distance away from the aerodrome – its silt bed possibly still riddled with those rusting bullets to this very day.

OFFENSIVE PATROLS

On 22 January Major Read returned after his brief absence and resumed command of No.45 Squadron. Intriguingly, the squadron record book relates that he was involved in a 'special mission' that morning with Lieutenant Mullery acting as his observer in Sopwith 7794. Squadron commanders were forbidden from flying into hostile territory – something that was a source of great frustration to Major Read – and so whatever this special mission was, it is unlikely to have involved flying over the German lines.

That same afternoon Joseph flew with Captain Williams in 7794 as part of a four-aircraft reconnaissance flight to Lille. The following day, 23 January, the pair flew again and Joseph took part in his first offensive patrol. Upon returning to the aerodrome, the two men submitted a written account of what happened during this flight.[23] Their handwritten notes were typed into the following combat report:

Combats in the Air

Date: 23.1.17
Time: 12.15–12.35pm
Duty: Offensive Patrol
Height: 10,000
Squadron: No.45 Squadron R.F.C.
Type and No. of aeroplane: Sopwith 2/Str: A/1083
Armament: 1 Vickers & 1 Lewis Gun
Pilot: Capt. W.G.B. Williams
Observer: 2/Lt. J. Senior
Locality: Over MENIN

Remarks on Hostile machine:-Type, armament, speed, etc.
No particulars of first H.A.
Second H.A. Halberstadt with green planes and black crosses.
Third H.A.   do.   do.   do.

Narrative

Saw 1 H.A. type unknown about 1,000 feet beneath us just E. of the FORET D'HOUTHULST. Dived on him from about 10,000 feet to 8,000 feet firing on him with front gun, when he put his nose down and went straight for the ground. Unable to say whether H.A. was hit owing to lack of tracer in belt.

Met 2nd H.A. going S. just N. of MENIN; saw him about 800 yards away and came to within 400 yards of him. Opened fire with front gun, when H.A. turned E. we turned S.E. and got Lewis Gun to bear on him over top plane. H.A. which was very fast and slightly higher, then outdistanced us and dived towards ground. Some of

---

23 All combat reports in this chapter are extracted from TNA AIR 1/1786/204/151/1. In some instances the handwritten reports have survived alongside their typed counterparts.

our tracers seemed to be hitting him.

About 5 minutes later saw another H.A. diving on to the rear of the formation. Opened fire on him with Lewis Gun at a range of 300 yards decreasing to 100 yards. H.A. then dived in between leader and rear machines and went straight down. Lost sight of him after about 2000 feet owing to plane. This H.A. was certainly hit by our tracer in the engine and in the fuselage.

(sd)   W.G.B. Williams, Capt. (Pilot)

(sd)   J. Senior, 2/Lt. (Observer)

The first thing to note about this combat report is that 'do' is a contracted form of *'ditto'* and is used here to indicate that the second and third enemy aircraft were both identified as being Halberstadts. Identification of the first enemy aircraft proved impossible (possibly due to the swift evasive action it took after being fired upon) and lack of tracers in the pilot's Vickers gun belt meant that Williams was unable to say for certain whether he had hit it.

Tracers were a special type of bullet, loaded at regular intervals in the machine-gun belt, which left a phosphorescent trail through the air. They enabled the gunner to see clearly the trajectory of his bullets, and also to make aiming adjustments. There is a note pencilled in the margin of the original typed combat report which asks the question: 'why no tracer?' This was quite possibly a question that Major Read asked of whoever was responsible for loading the bullets into the Vickers gun belt. Joseph's Lewis gun belt did contain tracer bullets and some of these seemed to hit the second enemy aircraft, although they do not appear to have caused critical damage. Joseph reports having far greater success with the third hostile aircraft, which he fired upon as it approached A/1083 from the rear – causing the enemy aircraft to plummet out of control. The corresponding squadron record book entry is reproduced below and details all four Sopwiths involved in this aerial encounter:

No.45 Squadron record book entry – 23 January 1917

| 7794 | 2/Lt. Garratt | Offensive Patrol | 11.15–12.55 |
| | 2/Lt. Carey | (2 H.A. seen) | |

A/1083	Capt. Williams 2/Lt. Senior	Offensive Patrol (2 H.A. met and fired at. Both guns working well)	11.10–12.55
7774	Lt. Hamilton Gnr. Lambert	Offensive Patrol (2 H.A met and fired at with rear gun. Engine unsatisfactory oil pipe broken)	11.10–12.55
7792	2/Lt. Courtney 2/Lt. Northcote	Offensive Patrol (Landed at No.1. Aerodrome BAILLEUL. Observer wounded in leg. Engine and petrol tank hit by H.A. Gun fire)	11.10–12.15

Second Lieutenant Northcote was evidently wounded during this offensive patrol, as a result of which his pilot (Courtney) landed at Bailleul in order for him to receive medical treatment. No.45 Squadron had its own doctor, but Bailleul was closer to where the aerial combat had taken place and had medical facilities in Bailleul Asylum, which was situated next to No.1 Squadron Aerodrome. It is interesting to note that Captain Williams took a test flight to Bailleul later that same afternoon, with Joseph as his observer, and, although not recorded in the squadron record book, it seems likely that they visited Northcote in his hospital bed whilst there.

Contemporary postcard image of the administration block of Bailleul Asylum

Bailleul had been a British garrison town since 15 October 1914, when the British had liberated it from the Germans. Located approximately 10 miles to the east of Sainte-Marie-Cappel, and a similar distance from the front, it was an important base for Army and RFC operations. There were three aerodromes here, which were all located to the east of the town. No.1 Squadron Aerodrome was the northernmost of the three and was next to the asylum. 'The Asylum Aerodrome', as it was sometimes known, covered an area of 55 acres and features regularly in the No.45 Squadron record book. 23 January is the first recorded incident of Joseph visiting Bailleul. It would not be his last.

PHOTOGRAPHIC PATROLS

The cameras used for aerial photography were very basic in comparison to modern devices. Essentially large, wooden boxes, they had a handle on top for changing the photographic plates and a cord that had to be pulled to make the exposure. Handheld cameras were generally used for taking oblique photographs, whilst vertical photographs were taken using fixed cameras. These vertical cameras were either fitted to the side of the fuselage or fixed inside the aircraft. By the end of February 1917, holes had been cut in the rear cockpit floors of No.45 Squadron's Sopwiths in order to facilitate the use of their vertical cameras. Their correct operation required a great deal of concentration on the part of the observer, whose job it was to take the photographs.

On the morning of 24 January, Joseph took his first aerial photographs of enemy positions. Flying in A/1075 with Captain Williams as his pilot, the pair were escorted by three others aircraft from their squadron. There should have been a four-aircraft escort for this patrol, but Lieutenant Hamilton experienced engine problems shortly after take-off and had to return 7774 to the aerodrome. Escort planes were often critical to the success of photographic missions as their role was to protect the photography plane from enemy fire. This was important as the observer's full attention was on exposing his photographic plates, whilst his pilot was focussed on keeping the aircraft steady above the target area. Fortunately, on this particular occasion, only one hostile aircraft was seen and this was on the British side of the line as they were returning. Unfortunately, Joseph's camera went wrong over enemy-held Roubaix and a petrol pipe broke on the way home, causing Captain Williams to land at Bailleul. That afternoon further photography practice was undertaken by Joseph, presumably to ensure his camera was now working properly.

Below is an undated aerial photograph that appears in Joseph's photograph album. The location is not revealed in the album, but the landscape is unmistakably that of Ypres. This can be positively affirmed from the distinctive moat which winds its path around the town's ramparts. Ypres would later become famous as the location of the Menin Gate Memorial, a lasting tribute to the British soldiers with no known graves who gave their lives to defend it. The position of the Menin Gate can be pinpointed in this photograph by tracing the eastern section of the moat northwards until it intersects with the road leading away from it to the east.

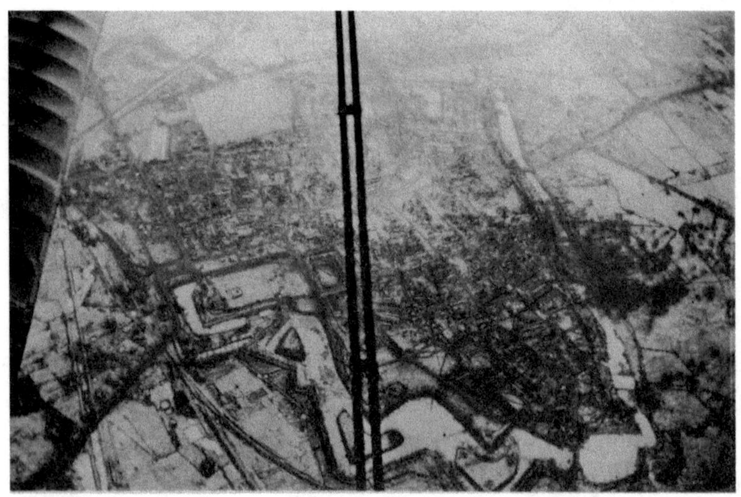

Aerial photograph of Ypres, taken from Sopwith 1½ Strutter (Author's collection)

On 25 January, Joseph flew with Captain Williams as one of four escorts on a mission to photograph the area from Becelaere to Courtrai. The photography plane was piloted by Captain Mackay, with Second Lieutenant Austin acting as his observer. This mission was recalled three times due to Austin's camera being out of order. Finally, on his fourth attempt, Austin managed to expose 18 plates before his camera went wrong again. Upon returning to base, all four escort planes reported seeing trains moving south from Courtrai towards Menin. These train movements may well have indicated the transportation of enemy troops into the area, information that would have been passed on to British ground forces.

MENIN

Of all the enemy-held areas that No.45 Squadron flew above, Menin was arguably the most dangerous. Here pilots could expect a particularly hostile reception from ground-based anti-aircraft shelling and an equally hostile reception from predatory enemy aircraft. The resultant casualties were almost inevitable, as was the case on 26 January when six aircraft left Sainte-Marie-Cappel airfield on a photography mission:

No.45 Squadron record book entry – 26 January 1917

A/1076	Lt. McArthur	Photography	11.00–12.40
	2/Lt. Emery	(33 plates exposed)	
A/1075	Capt. Williams	Escort to photography	11.00–12.40
	2/Lt. Senior	(see combat report)	
A/2381	2/Lt. Campbell	Escort to photography	11.00–12.40
	2/Lt. Vessey	(see combat report)	
A/1083	2/Lt. Cock	Escort to photography	11.00–12.40
	2/Lt. Stewart	(see combat report)	
A/1071	Lt. Belgrave	Escort to photography	11.00–11.50
	Cpl. Jenkins	(Landed at Bailleul)	
A/1074	F/Sgt. Webb	Escort to photography	11.00–12.15
	Cpl. Fleming	(Missing)	

Flight Sergeant Webb and Corporal Fleming were later confirmed dead. Their fiery deaths were witnessed by other members of the mission, including Joseph, who submitted the following combat report:

Combats in the Air

Date: 26.1.17
Time: 12.00–12.15pm
Duty: Escort to photography
Height: 10,000 feet
Squadron: No.45
Type and No. of aeroplane: Sopwith 2/Str: A/1075

Armament: 1 Vickers 1 Lewis
Pilot: Capt. Williams
Observer: 2/Lt. J. Senior
Locality: N. of MENIN

Remarks on Hostile machine:-Type, armament, speed, etc.
2 Halberstadt: 1 white machine with extensions, thought to be
L.V.G. 1 Machine with struts, planes, rotary engine like a Nieuport,
fin and rudder like an Albatross Scout.

Narrative

Crossed the lines going due E. at PLOEGSTEERT in formation
of 5 machines. On the way out I was in one of the right hand
machines and saw a H.A. flying at about the same level as our
formation and in the same direction (E.) over in the neighbourhood
of TOURCOING. He gradually drew nearer and nearer to us, and
when about 400 yards away I saw that he was a Halberstadt and
opened fire on him with the Lewis Gun. Some of the tracers seemed
to be hitting him, but he immediately banked over to the right and
nose-dived towards the ground. I had noticed 3 machines following
our formation at about 12,000 feet after we crossed the lines and
after seeing the first mentioned machine go to the ground I kept a
watch on them. When we were just a little N.E. of MENIN, they
had almost overtaken us, and were still from 1,000 to 2,000 feet
higher than we and as the leading machine of our formation started
to turn, the 3 machines above us split up and started to dive in a fan
shape towards us. I at once opened fire with the Lewis Gun on the
machine that was on the side nearest to the lines but had to cease
fire owing to my own machine turning with the formation, with the
result that the top plane hid the H.A. from view. As we turned I saw
one of our own machines burst into flames. Almost at once the tail
plane fell away and the whole fell to the ground. At the same time
I noticed in the middle of our formation a machine which at first
sight seemed to be a Baby Nieuport. He was on the tail of one of
our machines and was firing at it so I turned the Lewis Gun on to

him at a range of about 400 yards and he turned to the S. and dived towards the ground. About 5 seconds later a white machine with black crosses passed over the top of us going in a N.E. direction. I opened fire on him with the Lewis and hit him several times in the fuselage, but had to turn my attention to another H.A. above us so did not see what happened to him.

(sd.)   J. Senior 2/Lt.
(Observer).

Joseph's room-mate, Second Lieutenant Cock, had a different perspective on the combat as he was flying at a higher altitude. His report, compiled with Lieutenant Stewart, contains the abbreviation 'H.A.A.' This stands for 'Hostile Anti-Aircraft'. These were the ground-based German artillery guns which were trained on the skies:

Combats in the Air

Date: 26.1.17
Time: 12.00–12.15pm
Duty: Escort to photography
Height: 10,500 feet
Squadron: No.45
Type and No. of aeroplane: Sopwith 2/Str. A/1083
Armament: 1 Vickers & 1 Lewis
Pilot: 2/Lt. G.H. Cock
Observer: 2/Lieut. C.G. Stewart
Locality: Over MENIN

Remarks on Hostile machine:-Type, armament, speed, etc.

2 Halberstadt. Presumably fixed M.G. Fast.

Narrative

From the time of leaving ARMENTIERES and up to the time when we were over the neighbourhood between TOURCOING and

MENIN, 1 H.A. was noticed flying low to our right. Towards MENIN he appeared to be climbing and edging towards our tail. The main hostile formation ahead was not visible to myself before the turn on account of our machine being higher than the rest of the formation, and nearly as high as the H.A., resulting in the top plane obscuring sufficient sky to cover their movements. Shortly before the turn I lost sight of the H.A. low right rear and on the turn whilst still searching for that machine, saw one of our own going to the ground in flames. The tail appeared to fall away from it. I attributed this calamity to H.A.A. at the time which had been shelling us previously. Almost immediately the outer H.A. of the main formation flew past at about 250 yards to our right on a steep bank and at great speed. I opened fire on this machine over the rudder, the turn preventing my so doing before he was nearly directly in rear. The tracers appeared to be going into the machine for the greater part of a very long burst at 300 yards; after which we appeared to gradually increase the distance between ourselves and the H.A.

> (sd.)   G.H. Cock 2/Lt. (Pilot)
> (sd.)   C.G. Stewart 2/Lt. (Observer)

Lieutenant McArthur was piloting the photography plane, with Second Lieutenant Emery acting as his observer and cameraman. Emery's report, in common with the others reproduced here, highlights the difficulties that were often experienced in correctly identifying enemy aircraft type. It is to be noted that the following combat report records McArthur's Sopwith as being A/1077, whereas the squadron record book entry records it as being A/1076:

Combats in the Air

Date: 26.1.17
Time: 12.15pm
Duty: Photography
Height: 10,000 feet
Squadron: No.45

Type and No. of aeroplane: Sopwith 2/Str; A/1077
Armament: 1 Fixed Vickers & 1 Lewis
Pilot: Lieut. L.W. McArthur
Observer: 2/Lieut. C.S. Emery
Locality: HALLUIN

Remarks on Hostile machine:-Type, armament, speed, etc.

3 machines seen, 1 H.A. on left flank at about 13,000 Type engaged not known, the pilot thinks that it was a Baby Nieuport but a fin was fitted. Pilot and self noticed rotary engine, because I saw my tracer go into it.

Narrative

I was taking photographs in the leading machine while going East towards COURTRAI. I saw 3 H.A. at about 14,000 behind us obviously waiting for us when we came back. After turning at COURTRAI between COURTRAI and MENIN E. of HALLUIN I was busy taking photographs and was therefore not aware that we were being attacked until I heard a regular fusillade behind and at our side. I was still taking photographs realising that the escort was engaging them when I looked to the right and saw one of our machines A/1074 drop in flames. The next moment my attention was distracted by having to take another photograph. Immediately this was done I turned round and saw a H.A. right in the middle of the formation on our tail and firing at us, so I thought that the best I could do was to try and damage him. I fired 97 rounds and saw my tracers hitting his engine and I saw him turn sharply. I then carried on with the photography. The Lewis Gun was firing perfectly though I only fired 97 rounds.

(sd.) C.S. Emery 2/Lt. (Observer.)

Major Read added the following handwritten note at the foot of Emery's report: 'This was a good performance undertaken in difficulties. The photographs were successful.' The Commonwealth War Graves Commission records the final resting places of the two airmen killed on this mission: Flight Sergeant Walter George Webb and Corporal Robert Dick Fleming are buried side-by-side at Menen Communal Cemetery in West-Vlaanderen, Belgium. Webb's age is not recorded, but Fleming was aged 22. The epitaph on his headstone contains the following words: 'Too dearly loved to be forgotten.'

LIEUTENANT L.W. MCARTHUR

Lawrence William McArthur was the son of a London stockbroker and his home address was in Chislehurst, Kent. Prior to joining the Royal Flying Corps, McArthur had served with the Honourable Artillery Company and it was whilst serving with this territorial unit that he had been awarded the Military Cross. His citation for the award appeared in *The London Gazette* (Issue 29240) and reads as follows: 'For conspicuous gallantry on June 16th 1915 at Hooge. When our troops were forced to retire from the 3rd line of German trenches he rallied part of the retiring troops and reoccupied and held the vacated trench under heavy fire until he was himself forced later to withdraw owing to retirements on his flanks. He was severely wounded on this occasion.'

As a result of his wounds, McArthur was shipped from Calais to Dover in order to convalesce back in England. A surviving medical record indicates that he was a second lieutenant at the time of his injury and aged 24. The same record relates that he had 'received a gun shot wound of the scalp and a small cut in the upper portion of the right parietal bone'. It was almost a year before he was deemed fit to return to active service, but on 31 May 1916 he satisfied the medical board and was seconded for duty with the Royal Flying Corps.[24] McArthur was one of the original pilots of No.45 Squadron to fly over to France in October 1916. He succeeded Captain Williams as commanding officer of 'C' Flight on 30 January 1917. This change in command was necessitated by the secondment of Williams to No.19 Squadron.

The earliest record of McArthur flying with Joseph is on 24 February 1917, when McArthur took A/2385 to the skies on a practice flight. Surviving records indicate that Joseph acted as McArthur's observer on 36 separate occasions, although the actual number is almost certainly higher than this as half the pages

---

24 The primary source material used in this chapter for McArthur's medical and military history comes from TNA WO 374/43517.

are missing from the April section of the squadron record book. McArthur features in Joseph's photograph album and is pictured below, in a photograph taken at Sainte-Marie-Cappel.

Lieutenant Lawrence William McArthur (Author's collection)

Joseph flew almost exclusively with McArthur from 24 February until 9 May 1917 and there are only three recorded occasions when he flew with other pilots during this time. The first of these three exceptions was on 26 February, when Joseph flew with Second Lieutenant James Edward Blake as escort on a photographic reconnaissance mission. This particular flight was abandoned, probably due to cloud, and is the only recorded incident of the pair flying together. The following day, Joseph carried out a line patrol with McArthur:

No.45 Squadron record book entry – 27 February 1917

A/2385   Lt. McArthur   Line Patrol   7.50–10.30
            2/Lt. Senior   (Clouds 5,000 feet.
                              No H.A. seen at 14,000 feet)

A/1074	2/Lt. Soloman	Line Patrol	7.50–10.15
	2/Lt. Selby	(Forced landing at DELETTE[S] 10 miles S. of ST. OMER. propeller broken and engine trouble. Not yet returned)	
7774	2/Lt. Cock	Line Patrol	7.50–10.15
	2/Lt. Stewart	(Forced landing near EBBLINGHEM. Not yet returned)	

Line patrols were generally less dangerous than offensive patrols because they did not involve penetration of enemy territory. However, as the above record entry indicates, they could still prove hazardous due to the unreliability of the machines the men were flying. On this particular occasion there were no casualties and Major Read, flying with Second Lieutenant Greenhow in A/1082, later managed to locate the two machines that had made forced landings.

Throughout March, Joseph's flying time was evenly distributed between line patrols and photographic reconnaissance. On 1 March, he successfully exposed 10 photographic plates whilst on reconnaissance over Comines and also recorded sighting a hostile kite balloon nearby. Kite balloons were large, sausage-shaped balloons, which were tethered to the ground and could be raised or lowered by means of a ground-based winch. A basket was suspended from the underside of the balloon and typically carried two men, whose job it was to observe enemy movements. Unlike airmen, these 'balloonatics' were provided with parachutes in case of emergency, although these did not guarantee a safe passage to earth due to the dangers of entanglement with the balloon's rigging.

Following his return from this reconnaissance mission, Joseph flew on a patrol with Lieutenant Alexander Evelyn Charlwood – during which he fired at a hostile aircraft above Steenwerke. This is the only recorded incident of the pair flying together.

PROMOTION

Joseph was promoted from second lieutenant to lieutenant sometime on or around 7 March 1917. His promotion coincided with that of Lieutenant McArthur, who became a captain. The squadron record book records that Captain McArthur and Lieutenant Senior took part in a photographic reconnaissance with four other aircraft on 9 March. This mission was abandoned owing to low cloud at 7,000 feet. Poor weather became a recurring feature for the rest of this month and led to many such flights being either recalled or abandoned.

On 15 March, Joseph flew with Cock on a practice flight. This was the last time that Joseph flew with Cock and for his remaining time with the squadron he flew exclusively with McArthur.

On 17 and 25 March, Joseph took part in two line patrols with McArthur. During the first of these patrols, the men reported seeing smoke rising from a large fire in Quesnoy and also in Ledeghem. On the latter occasion they reported seeing a fire at Messines. On 28 March, their photographic reconnaissance had to be abandoned due to clouds at 5,000 feet, and later that same day they had to return from another reconnaissance mission due to a cylinder cutting out.

'Bloody April'

The Royal Flying Corps suffered greater casualties in April 1917 than it had done in any previous month of the war. The Battle of Arras accounted for many of these casualties, but equally relevant was growing German air ascendancy. By this stage in the war, the Germans had developed aircraft which were superior to their British counterparts in terms of speed and manoeuvrability. No.45 Squadron, for instance, was still flying Sopwith 1½ Strutters and these machines were at a distinct disadvantage when compared to the latest German Albatros scouts. This factor, coupled with the RFC policy of keeping up a continuous air offensive, contributed to a huge spike in casualty figures – as demonstrated by the events of 6 April, when No.45 Squadron lost six men during a reconnaissance of Lille, Roubaix and Tournai. During this mission, the squadron's Sopwiths were ambushed by a combination of Halberstadt and Albatros scouts. These enemy aircraft engaged the reconnaissance formation at Tournai, just as the machines were making their homeward journey. In the resultant air combat, three Sopwiths were brought down and their respective crews declared missing. One of the missing men was Captain Brayshay, who was acting as observer to Second Lieutenant Blake in Sopwith 7806. There is a surviving letter detailing the circumstances of Brayshay's disappearance, which was sent to Mr A. Price later that same day. Brayshay was engaged to be married to Mr Price's daughter and had named his prospective father-in-law as his 'nearest of kin' because he wished his belongings to be forwarded to his fiancée in the event of his death.

The letter is addressed to 18 Wake Green Road, Moseley, Birmingham:

> Dear Mr Price,
>
> I am writing to tell you the sad news that Capt. Brayshay is missing whilst flying over the lines today.
>
> It is not certain but, I am afraid probable, that he was killed.
>
> Several of our machines were out on a reconnaissance together when they met some hostile machines. Two of our machines were in collision and fell to the ground near Tournai and one was seen to go down though not, it is thought, out of control – near Tournai also.
>
> This latter machine is believed to be the one in which Capt. Brayshay was flying though it is not certain and no one saw what eventually happened to this machine.
>
> I have questioned all those who saw what happened and I am inclined to think that there is little hope – though a very little – if this was Capt. Brayshay's machine. I am trying to find out by dropping a message over the lines – what happened to him and I will inform you if I hear anything. If there is any hope it usually comes through within three months.
>
> I am sending home to you via the D.A.G. Base, all Capt. Brayshay's personal belongings – since it is you who he put down as his "nearest of kin". His kit I will also send to you via Messrs Cox & Co's Officer's Kit Department.
>
> Yours sincerely
>
> (Sgd.) W.R. Read
>
> (Major Comdg. No.45 Sqdn. R.F.C.)[25]

The two Sopwiths which collided with one another were A2381 (Second Lieutenant Colin St. George Campbell/Captain Donald William Edwards) and A1093 (Lieutenant John Arthur Marshall/Lieutenant Francis George Truscott).

---

25 This letter (a copy of the original) is to be found within TNA WO 374/8721. Their copy contains a repeated misspelling of Brayshay's surname (appearing as 'Brayshaw'), which I have corrected in my transcription as it is clearly a typing error.

All four airmen were killed outright. The third machine (Sopwith 7806) managed a controlled descent and both Brayshay and Blake survived the landing. They were, however, to die shortly afterwards as prisoners of war, having succumbed to their injuries. The anxiety caused by Blake's disappearance is apparent from a surviving letter written by his girlfriend. The following letter was sent to the War Office on 13 July 1917 from the Kings Head Hotel, High Street, Chatham, Kent:

> Dear Sir,
>
> I should be so glad if you could give me any information about 2nd Lieutenant J. E. Blake, 45th Squadron, R.F.C., B.E.F. France. Last April I had a letter, which I had written to him, returned to me, with a note inside, from an officer who stated that he was a friend of Lieut. Blake's, saying:- "This officer's machine was seen to come down behind the German Lines, apparently under control". – Since receiving that note, I have had no further letters from Lieut. Blake neither have I seen any report shewing him as "killed".
>
> Apologising for troubling you and thanking you in anticipation.
> Yours Sincerely
> Elsie Revill

The War Office replied to Miss Revill's letter two days later, informing her that no further news had been received concerning Second Lieutenant Blake since his disappearance.[26] Miss Revill was also informed that 'should any further report be received, it will be communicated to the Officer's father who is registered as his next-of-kin.'

Confirmation of Blake's death eventually came via a message dropped from a German aeroplane flying over the British lines. The Germans also confirmed the deaths of the other missing airmen, including Lieutenant Francis George Truscott. Truscott receives a mention in a letter Joseph wrote to his father on Easter Monday. The date of Easter varies each year according to the lunar cycle and always occurs following a full moon. In 1917 Easter Monday fell on 9 April, a fact confirmed by Joseph's reference to Truscott being lost on Good Friday (6 April) and reinforced by his reference to moonlight:

---

26 Both these letters are to be found within TNA WO 339/59987.

Easter Monday

My dear Father

Thank you very much for the parcel, which arrived safely the other afternoon. We have been very busy lately so far as the weather has permitted, & consequently have had to pay the penalty, witness our contributions to the latest Rolls of Honour. It's a very welcome thing to know that people at home are beginning to make an agitation about Flying Corps matters, because there's more than good reason for it. However, I suppose we shall have to carry on as we are until they can supply us with more up-to-date machines. We feel particularly sore about it just now, because we've lost several good fellows of late, including Truscott on Good Friday morning. You will remember that he came with Moore & myself to 45 Squadron from the 4th Corps Cyclist Bn last October & we miss him very much, because he was always so cheery & one of the straightest fellows I've ever known. Yesterday, Easter Sunday, was a delightful spring day, now the weather's changed round again & we're getting blizzards of hail & sleet. An old Hun came over here the other night evidently with the intention of doing a little of the Zep business, but couldn't find us, because he didn't loose off any of his cargo, & yet he was so low down that we were able to make him out in the moonlight. Can't you imagine us all standing out on the duckboards in pyjamas, watching him with great interest? I think I realise now something of what a Zep night in England must be, except that there were no searchlights, but Archie was blazing away into the night & lighting up the sky with his gun-flashes.
My best love to all
Your affectionate son
Joseph

Truscott had been educated at Rugby School and his obituary is one of many featured in Philip Lee Warner's *Memorials of Rugbeians who fell in the Great War: Volume IV* (Rugby: The Medici Society, 1918). This book includes snippets of three condolence letters sent to Truscott's family by fellow RFC officers. One of these unnamed officers wrote: 'His was a life for which England in particular and the world in general were very much the better. With us he was ever the cheeriest of friends, straight and true as gold; one feels it a privilege to have known him.'[27]

In the final part of Joseph's letter there is a reference to 'Archie'. This was slang for 'anti-aircraft fire' and was reputedly derived from an old music hall song called 'Archibald, Certainly Not!' Today a version of this humorous song can be found on the internet, but in Joseph's day recordings could only be heard on gramophone players. There was a gramophone player in the flight mess of No.45 Squadron, but whether or not this particular song was ever played can only be guessed.

Below is a picture from Joseph's photograph album which seems best to evoke the 'Zep[pelin] business' of his letter. All three men in this photograph are in various states of dress and the man in the centre is clearly wearing slippers, his fur coat quite possibly concealing white pyjamas.

Three unidentified airmen of No.45 Squadron standing on duckboards. The man in the middle is believed to be Second Lieutenant Norman Macmillan. If this identification is correct, then the picture is likely to have been taken in early April 1917 (Author's collection)

---

27 'Memorials of Rugbeians' also features a picture of Truscott, from which it has been possible to identify him in Joseph's photograph album.

VAN RYNEVELD

In mid-April 1917, No.45 Squadron moved its personnel to a second site at Sainte-Marie-Cappel. This move was necessitated by the arrival of No.20 Squadron, which was henceforth to share the same airfield. In order to accommodate this new squadron, Joseph's squadron were ordered to vacate their Nissen sleeping huts and exchange them for tents in a nearby meadow. This enforced move did not go down well with the men of No.45 Squadron. Later that same month, Major Read decided to leave the RFC altogether and return to his previous regiment, the Dragoon Guards. His replacement was Major H.A. van Ryneveld, who had been born in the Orange Free State and would later become instrumental in establishing the South African Air Force.

Van Ryneveld became the CO of No.45 Squadron on 24 April 1917, a fact confirmed by the appearance of his signature in the squadron record book entry for that day. That same morning, Joseph flew with McArthur on a reconnaissance in which six hostile aircraft were encountered west of Roulers. One machine was seen to go down in flames. Cock also took part in this reconnaissance, flying with Murison as his observer, and he reported seeing 10 hostile aircraft. In the afternoon, Joseph and McArthur took part in a northern patrol which had to be curtailed due to weather conditions. This uneventful patrol is noteworthy because McArthur was flying a French-built Nieuport 20 aircraft (serial number A/6731), rather than a Sopwith 1½ Strutter. McArthur had fetched this particular Nieuport from No.1 Aircraft Depot at Saint-Omer on 13 April and it was one of a small batch of Nieuports that were allocated to the squadron as a stopgap measure whilst waiting for replacement Strutters to be built back in England. In common with the Sopwith Strutter, the Nieuport was a two-seater aircraft, but it was much slower and less responsive. Second Lieutenant Norman Macmillan also flew a Nieuport in this abandoned patrol, flying in A/6740 with 2/AM Shaw as his observer. Macmillan had joined No.45 Squadron on 31 March 1917 and he later published his wartime experiences in a book: *Into the Blue* (first published by Gerald Duckworth & Co, 1929).

JOSEPH'S FINAL MISSIONS

On the morning of 2 May, Captain McArthur piloted Joseph in one of two photography planes. The other photography plane was piloted by Captain Jenkins with Second Lieutenant Austin acting as his observer. There were initially seven escorts assigned to this mission, but this was reduced to six when Second Lieutenant Carleton's plane had to return to base due to a misfiring engine. Once over the enemy lines, the formation engaged with several camouflaged enemy scouts. The squadron record book reveals a familiar pattern of Lewis guns jamming and aircraft engines misfiring, but on this occasion there were no casualties. Both photography planes were successfully protected by their escorts and returned safely to base with photographs of the target area. Austin had only been able to expose one plate before his camera jammed, but Joseph had better luck and successfully exposed 27 plates. That afternoon Joseph and McArthur took part in an offensive patrol with many of the same men who had flown in the morning, this time with no opposition.

At 9:30 a.m. on 3 May, Joseph took part in an eight-aircraft northern patrol, flying as observer to McArthur in A/2385. An hour into this flight McArthur had to tail off from the rest of the formation and land his machine at No.1 Aircraft Depot due to a leaking petrol pipe. Captain Jenkins, flying in Sopwith 7803, also had to return to base due to engine trouble. The remaining Sopwiths encountered a small number of enemy aircraft, who were reluctant to engage in aerial combat. Curiously, Belgrave and Stewart reported seeing a small, scarlet, pear-shaped balloon floating over Poperinge at 12,000 feet, with nothing apparently attached to it and six feet in diameter. Furthermore, Lieutenant Charlwood reported that his observer, Second Lieutenant Carey, fainted in the air after a violent attack of vomiting. Carey would later act as observer to McArthur and, although the reasons for his airborne illness are not explained in the squadron record book, it seems likely that he was suffering from 'the effects of excessive flying' – a phrase used by Joseph in his last surviving letter.

At 11:15 a.m. McArthur flew back to Sainte-Marie-Cappel from No.1 Aircraft Depot, the leaking petrol pipe on A/2385 having been fixed. At 2:00 p.m. he swapped aircraft and took A/991 to the air on a southern offensive patrol, during which Joseph exposed 10 photographic plates. Sergeant Cook flew the repaired A/2385 on the same patrol, but reported further engine problems and returned before the patrol had been completed. On his return, Cook caught sight of one hostile aircraft at 14,000 feet above Clairmarais, which he chased over the lines. Lieutenant Charlwood also took part in this patrol with Second Lieutenant Selby acting as replacement observer for Carey, who was presumably receiving medical treatment. Charlwood also reported engine problems and these prevented him from keeping up with the rest of the formation.

On 4 May, Joseph acted as observer to McArthur on a northern offensive patrol with seven other aircraft, three of which had to return prematurely with engine problems. The remaining machines encountered six enemy aircraft, which they managed to chase away. Joseph successfully exposed 14 photographic plates on this mission, and a further 10 plates were exposed by Second Lieutenant Stewart, acting as observer to Lieutenant Belgrave. Two days after this patrol, Joseph wrote a letter to his brother George. In this letter, Joseph makes reference to the change of accommodation necessitated by the arrival of No.20 Squadron the previous month. He also reveals his aspiration to become a pilot one day. To the author's knowledge, this is the last letter that Joseph ever wrote:

6 May 17

My dear George

How are you faring in these days? I'm thinking that your time at the Divisional School must be about up now, & so I'm addressing this to the Bn.

With any luck I shall be going on 10 days' leave next Sunday, & I'm more than ready for it. This fine weather has put us absolutely in the soup, & we're all feeling the effects of excessive flying. At the same time, it's rendered our tent-dwelling very much more pleasant. We've ceased to regret our wooden huts on the other side of the aerodrome.

The cinema man came our way the other day & took our pictures: so I shall be very interested to see the War Films, when I'm on leave.

I'm very hopeful that it won't be long after my leave, when they send me home to learn to fly: it's just about time that I did go, but at present there seems to be a great shortage of observers, & they're keeping us back longer than the usual period.

Write soon.

Joseph

The Imperial War Museum is custodian to many war films produced during the

Great War. Amongst its collection is a film entitled 'With the Royal Flying Corps (Somewhere in France)'. This silent black & white film runs for approximately 15 minutes and can be viewed online at film.iwmcollections.org.uk. The film catalogue number is IWM 141 and it is summarised on the website as 'The RFC base at Sainte Marie Cappel, Western Front, late August 1917.' Despite this description, the film contains footage taken prior to August and includes a section filmed sometime between 20 April and 6 May 1917. This can be deduced from the presence of Nieuport A/6741 on the airfield as it was on loan to No.45 Squadron during this specific period, after which it was returned to No.1 Aircraft Depot. A/6741 can be briefly glimpsed in the section of the film entitled 'Setting out on an offensive patrol' which occurs 11 minutes into the film. Next to the grounded Nieuport can be seen Sopwith A/1083 about to take off, with the serial numbers of the other planes being illegible. The IWM website refers to A/1083 as being the aircraft usually flown by Second Lieutenant Cock and, given the supporting dating evidence, it can be stated with near certainty that this is the film that Joseph is referring to when he writes: 'the cinema man came our way the other day & took our pictures.' It is therefore wholly conceivable that Joseph's plane appears in this film amongst those lined up on the airfield. Sadly, if he was ever filmed, Joseph never had the opportunity to see himself on the big screen. Just three days after writing to George, he took part in his final flight with No.45 Squadron. Joseph is pictured below, standing beside Sopwith A/8226, in a photograph that was taken sometime between 25 April and 9 May 1917. This is almost certainly the last photograph that was ever taken of him.

Joseph standing next to Sopwith A/8226 (Image © Cross & Cockade International)

No.45 Squadron record book entry – 9 May 1917[28]

A/9632/	Lt. Johnstone	S. Offensive Patrol	3.20–6 .20
	2/AM Harries	(4 H.A. seen & fired at. 1 shot down out of control. See Report)	
7803	Lt. Mills	S. Offensive Patrol	3.20–
	2/AM Loughlin	(Missing)	
A/8260	2/Lt. Cock	S. Offensive Patrol	3.20–6.15
	2/Lt. Murison	(Combat with 4 H.A. & 11 H.A. Pilot shot down 1 H.A. with front gun (out of control). Observer shot 1 H.A. down within 50 ft. of machine which folded up after falling 100 feet.)	
A/8226	Capt. McArthur	S. Offensive Patrol	3.20 –
	Lt. Senior	(Landed at No.1 Aerodrome. Observer wounded fatally)	
A/991	Lt. Charlwood	S. Offensive Patrol	3.20–6.05
	2/Lt. Selby	(Encounter with 4 Albatross Scouts. 2 were driven down and disappeared into clouds)	
A/8225	2/Lt. Wright	S. Offensive Patrol	3.20–6.15
	2/Lt. C-Kelly	(Encounter with 4 H.A. In co-operation with another machine shot down 1 H.A. which fell to pieces near the ground. *The other machine was probably 7803*)	

---

28 The No.45 Squadron record book entry for 9 May 1917 is missing. Thankfully however, there is an existent continuation entry for 10 May which completes the final entries of the previous day. Rather confusingly, this continuation entry lists the start time for the previous day's patrol as being '6.00', which is clearly wrong given the corresponding return times. I have amended this start time here to read '3.20', based on the British loss report of Sopwith 7803 – which gives this as the start time of the patrol. The reason for the start-time 'error' in the record book seems to have been because 6:00 p.m. was the deadline for making entries, regardless of whether all the machines had returned by this time – and the continuation entry simply refers back to when the last entry was made. Consequently, the return-time entry for the missing page of 9 May is likely to have read '6.00' with the remarks column recording 'not yet returned'.

There are two surviving combat reports relating to this offensive patrol, the first of which was submitted by Cock and Murison:

Combats in the Air

Date: May 9th 1917
Time: 4.50pm
Duty: Offensive Patrol
Height: about 10,000 feet
Squadron: No.45
Type and No. of aeroplane: Sopwith 2/Str: A/8260
Armament: 1 Vickers 1 Lewis
Pilot: 2/Lt. Cock
Observer: Lt. J.T.G. Murison
Locality: N.W. SECLIN

Remarks on Hostile machine:-Type, armament, speed, etc.

Single seater painted grey with distinct iron cross painted black on fuselage, fin and wings.
4 machines in formation.
30 machines about WERVICQ AND MENIN.

Narrative

When on an Offensive Patrol about N.W. of SECLIN, we observed 4 H.A.'s flying in formation towards our rear, we immediately fired a red light and attacked reaching the H.A.'s sometime before the rest of our formation. The pilot fired at 2 H.A. at a range of about 120 yards (using his Aldis Sight); one of the H.A.'s was observed to dive and then spin and fall completely out of control. The pilot 2/Lt. Cock then manoeuvred quickly so as to allow the observer to use his gun on the remaining 3 H.A. who were then diving upon us. One of them was hit right in his centre section by a burst of about 80 rounds at a distance of 50 feet. The H.A. immediately collapsed and was followed down by bursts of fire for about 100 feet when it completely folded up and went to pieces. We then returned to our lines to regain formation.

(sd.)   G.H. Cock, 2/Lt. (Pilot)
(sd.)   J.T.G. Murison Lt. (Observer)

A different perspective on this air battle is offered by Wright and Caulfield-Kelly, who submitted the following combat report:

Combats in the Air

Date: May 9th 1917
Time: 5.30pm
Duty: Offensive Patrol
Height: 12,000 feet
Squadron: No.45
Type and No. of aeroplane: Sopwith 2/Str: A/8225
Armament: 1 Vickers 1 Lewis
Pilot: 2/Lt. Wright
Observer: 2/Lt. E.T. Caulfield-Kelly
Locality: FOURNES

Remarks on Hostile machine:-Type, armament, speed, etc.
4 Albatross Scouts
11 Albatross Scouts

Narrative

The formation crossed the lines halfway between ARMENTIERES and LA BASSEE and when about 6 miles over 4 H.A. were seen climbing from direction of SECLIN 3 in formation and 1 well above. They were first seen by the rear machine which fired a red light and our machine followed it, passing under the H.A. The rear gun on our machine together with another machine of our formation now got in a full drum at the nearest H.A. which fell for a great distance in a spin and then fell to pieces near the ground. (His tail fell off). Another of the H.A. had previously been shot down out of control by the front gun of one of our machines and the remaining one of the 3 in formation dived away; the fourth machine did not come down near our formation. Formation now recrossed the lines and reformed crossing again over ARMENTIERES and going NORTH across LILLE towards MENIN. 11 H.A. were seen near MENIN coming towards formation. The formation attacked them and got separated, one machine remaining with us at about 1,000 feet higher. One H.A. with red tail dived on our machine and the other machine of our formation dived on it. We manoeuvred out of the way and saw 2 other H.A. diving on our other machine. I emptied half a drum into the nearest of these and my Lewis Gun then jammed and we had to return across the lines.

> (sd.)   W.A. Wright 2/Lt. (Pilot)
> (sd.)   E.T. Caulfield-Kelly (Observer)

Norman Macmillan also makes reference to this aerial encounter in his book 'Into the Blue'. Macmillan relates that the Sopwith patrol was met by Albatros scouts from Jasta 28. These enemy aircraft had taken off from Marcke-sur-Lys, between Courtrai and Menin, and the two opposing forces had clashed between Menin and Warneton. Lieutenant Mills died as a result of wounds sustained in the subsequent aerial combat and in the ensuing crash his observer, 2/AM Loughlin, was thrown clear of 7803 and taken prisoner of war. Macmillan has this to say about Sopwith A/8226: 'McArthur got away, partly through his flying skill, partly through the heroism of his observer who, although mortally wounded and with his right hand partially shot away, continued firing with his left hand and drove the nearest scout down.'[29]

There are no surviving combat reports for Jasta 28, but two other relevant German sources have survived: the *Nachrichtenblatt der Luftstreitkräfte* (intelligence report of the German Air Force); and the *Kommandeur der Flieger 4 Armee* (Air Commander report of the German 4 Army on the Ypres sector – commonly abbreviated to Kofl 4). These two sources confirm the fact that only two German pilots claimed 'victories' in the Ypres sector on 9 May 1917 – both against Sopwiths. These two pilots served with Jasta 28: *Oberleutnant* (Lieutenant) Karl Emil Schäfer and *Vizefeldwebel* (Sergeant

---

29 Macmillan, 'Into the Blue', p.95.

Major) Kurt Wittekind. The *Nachrichtenblatt* records Schäfer's claim as being over Warneton, and Wittekind's claim is recorded as being in the vicinity of 'Wytschaetebogen' – loosely referring to the Messines Ridge. The Kofl 4 report further distinguishes between these two claims by describing Schäfer's as being *diesseits* – that is to say 'on this side' of the German lines; and Wittekind's as being *jenseits* – that is to say 'beyond' the German lines. Given the fact that 2/ AM Loughlin was taken prisoner of war by the Germans, it can be deduced that Schäfer was responsible for shooting down Sopwith 7803. It therefore follows that Wittekind was responsible for the bullets that hit A/8226. The Kofl 4 report names 'Ploegsteert Wald' as the specific location of Wittekind's claim. This wood (named 'Plug Street Wood' by the British) seems to have been where Wittekind broke off his attack, possibly believing that the Sopwith he had hit was about to crash. It seems likely, given the accuracy of his shooting, that Wittekind was close enough to see his bullets hitting Joseph in the rear cockpit. The time of this combat is recorded as being 19:00, i.e. 7:00 p.m. This can be corrected to read 6:00 p.m. since German time was one hour ahead of British time throughout May 1917.

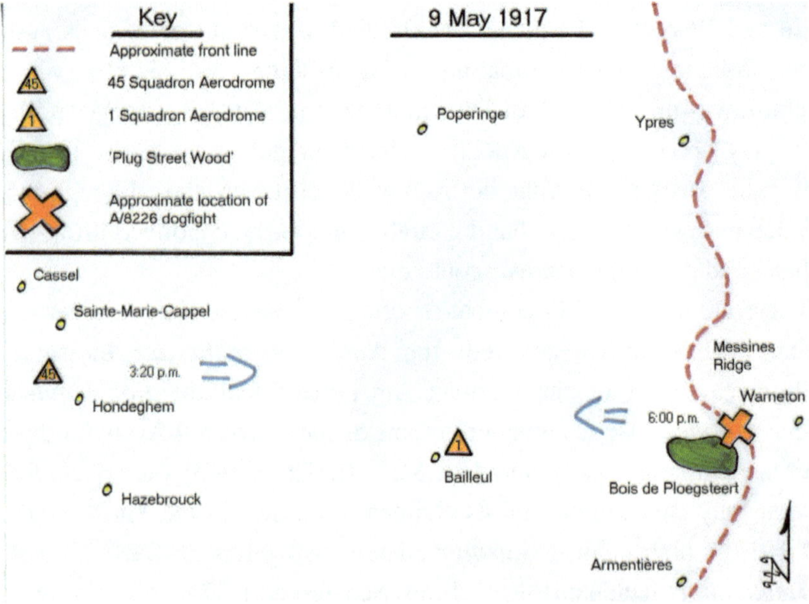

Map showing approximate location of A/8226 dogfight

On 10 May, a day after the aerial combat, a telegram was sent from the War Office to Arthur, mistakenly addressed to his former residence at 'Normandale' on Bradford Road in Wakefield:

Regret to inform you Lt J. Senior R.F.C. admitted fifty three Casualty Clearing Station with gunshot wound abdomen hand and leg seriously wounded.

A day later, on 11 May, another telegram was sent:

Deeply regret to inform you Lieut J. Senior R.F.C. 45 Sqd Died of Wounds May ninth. The Army Council express their sympathy.

These two telegrams elicited the following response from Joseph's father:

> Manygates Park,
> Sandal. Wakefield
> 11th May 1917

The Secretary of war

Sir, I am in receipt of your two telegrams today. The first one received about 9.30 am to inform me that my son was seriously wounded the second about 3.30 pm says my son died of wounds on the 9th inst. I shall wait fuller details.

Upon receipt of the first telegram I wired to my third son 2Lieut Geo[rge] Senior 4 K.O.Y.L.I. – attached 2/6 Sherwood Foresters France, asking him to try to see his brother. My second son 2Lieut W.T. Senior was reported 'missing' at Thiepval 3rd of Sept last.

I am quite broken.

Please send any further communications as above which is my present address.

Yours Truly

Arthur Senior.

Of all the letters that appear in this book, this is perhaps the most poignant. In four words Arthur sums up his feeling of devastation. Many condolence letters were sent to Arthur following the death of his eldest son – the first of these was written by Joseph's pilot, Captain McArthur. It provides a detailed account of Joseph's final hours:

Thursday,
May 10th, 1917.

Dear Mr Senior,

Your poor boy Joe died at 10.30 last night of wounds received about 6.o'clock in the afternoon (Wednesday May 9th). This is the most appalling news to have to send you and struck as I feel myself it cannot be a fraction of what you and his poor Mother must feel.

We were leading an offensive patrol and spotting a hun I dived on him. We pursued him down a considerable distance and he went for the ground. We had hardly turned round to make for home, when (as far as I can make out) about three other Huns got on our tail. There was a lot of firing which I evaded several times by turning the machine as quickly as possible, but after the second or third burst which hit our machine, Joe told me down the telephone that he had had one finger smashed and that he thought he was hit in the stomach. This sounded very bad, but I was cheered to hear him speaking in his usual perfectly calm way.

The Huns still came on and I thought the only thing to do was to turn and twist and avoid them as much as possible, when to my astonishment I suddenly heard Joe firing his gun again. It really was amazing.

We eventually got back and I went straight down to the nearest aerodrome to the lines, where I knew there was a hospital adjoining.

When we had landed, Joe said in his matter of fact way – "Well I think they'll have to lift me out, I don't feel as though I can get out alone." I could hardly believe he was so bad. The only sign of pain he gave was to encourage me to get down as quickly as possible, but his calm courage, with never a complaint, while he was being put on the stretcher and going into the Hospital, made me think he was certainly going to pull through all the time. I saw him into the receiving room where we had time for a short chat and he seemed comfortable and wanted nothing. I said that his keeping on firing had saved us, and he smiled and said he hoped we had hit one of them. It is dreadful to find now that it has only saved me. The doctors came in almost immediately and I said "Tata – I'll be back again directly to see how you're getting on" – He smiled and said "Cheero"[30] – I came back in half an hour (this would be about 7.30) expecting to see him in bed probably, but they had decided to operate immediately and he was then undergoing the operation.

The Doctors told me then that he had a very severe abdominal wound and that there was very little hope. I went away again and then our C.O. Major Van Ryneveld arrived having brought our own Doctor (Geoghegan) along, whom he had sent straight to the hospital. Major V.R. and I then went round and Dr. Geoghegan came out of the theatre and told us they were still operating and that there was practically no hope. Major V.R. and I then went back to the Mess and Dr. Geoghegan said he would let us know how Joe came through the operation. Dr. G. came in about 8.45 and reported the operation finished (it lasted about an hour and a half), but that it was doubtful whether Joe would regain consciousness. He did not, and passed peacefully away at 10.30. The Doctors all said that the wound was so bad that everything would be numbed, so that he would not have suffered very badly. They told me also that his finger would not have had time to start being painful. I feel so sorry that I cannot give you any last message. I can only quote the few remarks I heard.

I can hardly imagine Joe knew his end was so near when I left him, as we were alone for a minute or two and I think he would have made some mention of it to me. I certainly never dreamt it could be so.

I think you may feel assured that everything possible was done for him. The ambulance was halfway across the aerodrome to meet us as we landed and not a moment was lost. At the time I did not realise the importance of this – However it was so. They are

---

30 'Cheero' was a common salutation used during the war. A further example of its usage can be found on a contemporary wallet amongst the IWM's online collection (catalogue number EPH 5507).

accustomed to dealing with urgent cases at this aerodrome with its adjacent hospital.

His loss here is mourned desperately by us all. He was the most perfect Gentleman one could meet. Amazing calm and courage on all occasions combined with perfect manners and such a delightful disposition.

I think I feel his loss as keenly as anyone here, as we used to see a good deal of each other. We went on leave together last February and have been flying together ever since. It is impossible to know exactly what happens in aerial fights etc, but many times I have attributed my safe keeping to his inexhaustible courage and skill, and then yesterday but for his extraordinary pluck we should have probably been shot down. I can no longer thank him as I have always been able to. I can only thank you for the most gallant observer I could ever have had. I hope to come home on leave soon, and if it would give you any consolation I should like to come and see you.

I can say nothing but ask you and his Mother to accept my deepest sympathy.

Yours very sincerely,
(signed) Lawrence W. Mc. Arthur.

Although not named in this letter, the hospital where Joseph was treated was Bailleul Asylum, which was adjacent to No.1 Squadron aerodrome. Another detail not included is the fact that McArthur had himself been wounded in this aerial encounter and subsequently needed treatment for an armour-piercing bullet which had punctured his heel. This resulted in him being sent home on a week's sick leave to recover. There is every reason to believe he kept his promise to visit Arthur during this leave. Details of Joseph's funeral are contained within the condolence letter of Major van Ryneveld, who had been Joseph's commanding officer for less than a month:

No 45. Sqdn. R.F.C.

B.E.F.

11th May, 1917.

Dear Mr Senior,

It is with the deepest regret and sympathy that I am writing to tell you of the death of your gallant son. He, with Capt. Mc. Arthur as pilot, together with five other machines were out – well over the lines – on what we call an offensive patrol.

Mc. Arthur and your son – the stoutest combination we had in the squadron – were leading the show, and they attacked about 15 Hun machines, and it was during the fight that ensued, that Senior was mortally wounded. They were well over the lines at the time, and after your son was hit, Mc. Arthur got very hard pressed indeed. Your son, however, kept on directing him and warning him of the Huns attacking from behind, and simply by splendid flying and coolness, Mc. Arthur got back over the lines, crossing them at only about 2,000 feet. They landed at the first aerodrome – one which has a hospital adjoining it. Your son was taken straight out of the machine into the hospital, and about an hour after landing they commenced the operation. From the beginning they held out very little hope, and he died without regaining consciousness at 10.30 p.m.

An oak coffin was made in our squadron together with a brass plate with the following inscription.

Lieut. Joseph Senior,

West Yorks & R.F.C.

Died of wounds,

May 9th, 1917.

He was buried at Bailleul cemetery at 8.30 a.m. this morning. Capt. J.D. Heath of No.53 C.C.S. was the officiating clergy-man, and there were eight Officers and twelve N.C.O's and men of the Squadron present at the funeral. Six of his flight Officers acting as the bearer party. Capt. Mc. Arthur, the Officers of "C" flight (your son's), the Officers of the Squadron and the men of the Squadron each gave a wreath.

A propeller cross is being made in the Squadron, and when it is erected, we will have a photo of the grave taken, and send you a copy. If possible also, we will try and take a photo from the air, to show the exact position of the grave.

Your son's kit is being sent to Messrs Cox & Co through the usual channels, and they will inform you when it arrives.

Capt. Mc. Arthur is going home on leave on the 12th inst, and he has promised to come and see you.

I will be only too glad to tell you anything further which you might wish to know.

With the Squadrons deepest sympathy.

Yours sincerely,

(signed) H.A. van Ryneveld.

(Comdg No 45 Sqdn.)

The squadron record book entry for the day of Joseph's funeral is missing and along with it the full list of men in attendance. Norman Macmillan does, however, appear to have been one of them: 'We buried [Senior] in Bailleul cemetery with the honour which his brave soul merited.'[31]

Joseph's propeller cross, referred to in Van Ryneveld's letter, was most likely constructed by the air mechanics or riggers of his squadron. It was common practice for members of the RFC to be commemorated in this way. Crosses were fashioned by cutting three blades of a propeller short and thrusting the remaining long blade into the earth. Covering the central hub was a metal plate, upon which was engraved the name of the deceased. Two early photographs of Joseph's propeller cross are shown below. Duckboards, a recurring feature of the Great War, can be seen in the background of the first of these.

---

31 Macmillan, 'Into the Blue', p.96.

Two photographs of Joseph's propeller cross (Author's collection)

The Condolence Letter of Geoffrey Cock

45. Squadron,
R.F.C.
B.E.F.
FRANCE.

13th May, 1917.

Dear Mr Senior,

I am writing to tell you how deeply we all sympathise with you about the death of your son Joe.

I had known him intimately for about six months, living together in the same hut and tent, and I cannot tell you how much I feel the loss of his cheery company.

He was a great favourite in the mess and was looked up to by the whole Squadron. He was the most perfect Gentleman and charming friend I ever knew. He put up a splendid fight against three hun machines who were attacking his machine, and although he had a bad internal wound, and had lost a finger, continued to fire his gun as long as there was a target to shoot at; typical of his wonderful calm courage.

He died a noble death.

Please accept the deep sympathy of myself and the mess with you in your bereavement.

Yours very sincerely,
G.H. Cock.

Second Lieutenant Cock was the third member of No.45 Squadron to send a condolence letter to Arthur. Cock is pictured below with Joseph (Cock on the left) in the tent they shared at Sainte-Marie-Cappel. This photograph was taken sometime between mid-April and early May 1917 – less than a month before Joseph's death.

Cock and Joseph in tent (Image © Cross & Cockade International)

The Condolence Letter of Matthew Peacock

21, Northmoor Road,
Oxford.
14th May, 1917.

Dear Mr Senior,

I cannot say how sorry my wife and I are to hear that poor Joe has met his death in the War, and that you are still without good news of Walter. I can assure you that I feel the loss of all these fine fellows terribly, and their number goes on increasing. I have heard of two others to-day – Usher and Fletcher.

We were delighted to see Joe when he came over from Cambridge, and to have Walter here so often when he was in training in Oxford and recently we have seen a good deal of George, and have been struck by his fine manly appearance. We sincerely hope that he will be spared to you.

Please accept our best thanks for your kindness in writing to tell us about your boys, whom I shall remember as long as I live, and also allow me to express our sincere sympathy with you and yours upon the sad losses that you have sustained – though I am still hopeful that Walter may be after all safe in the hands of the enemy.

Yours very truly,
(signed) Matthew H. Peacock.

Matthew Henry Peacock had been Head of Wakefield Grammar School from September 1883 until December 1910 and had therefore been Joseph's headmaster for the majority of his time at the school, Joseph having left in 1911. In his letter, Mr Peacock makes reference to Joseph having visited him in Oxford whilst he was studying Classics at Cambridge. He also makes reference to both Walter and George visiting him whilst in military training at Oxford. Two other old boys of Wakefield Grammar School also receive a mention in Mr Peacock's letter: 'Usher and Fletcher'. Second Lieutenant Robert William Armitage Usher (Lancashire Fusiliers) was a pupil of the school from 1901 until 1906. He was killed in France on 2 May 1917. Second Lieutenant Edward Stewart Fletcher (West Yorkshire Regiment) was a pupil of the school from 1908 until 1912. He was reported missing on 3 May 1917 and confirmed dead the following year.

The Condolence Letter of Joseph Barton

The Grammar School.
BRISTOL.
May, 1917.

Dear Mr Senior,

I do not feel able to express what is in my heart about your dear boy, whose friendship meant so much to us, and whose fineness of mind and character were among our intimate personal possessions. To utter the sympathy we feel for you is impossible, and the loss of a boy with whom we had lived in such delightful and perfect communion during all the years of his springtime and brilliant promise is more to us than can be suggested in words.

Time will never efface the gap which his departure leaves in our life: for the rare few, like him, can never be replaced, and only a man who finds his chief reward in life in the sympathy and response of such chosen spirits can realise what is meant when they pass from us. The only thing to thank God for is the perfect memory he leaves – always bright and untarnished, always the flower of May that nothing now can ever touch or spoil.

It is hardly conceivable that powers so clear as his, and sensibilities so far beyond the common, can in a moment be extinguished by a physical accident. A universe in which such a mind and character could be blotted out at a blow would not be a universe at all, but a chaos. He gave not only life, but all the hopes of a splendid career, and even when he was already a soldier, he was not content until he could face the greatest danger of all, and live with his life in his hands, day by day, for his country. So brave a soul, so modest and restrained in spite of his unusual attainments, has surely some other and wider destiny to fulfil, behind the veil which we cannot pierce.

Meanwhile we lose him, and the sense of that loss is so profound that it stupefies all powers of thought. He will always be dear and

living to me, and the privilege of having taught, known and loved him is a thing I shall cherish intensely and secretly while life lasts.
Yours ever sincerely,

(signed) J.E. Barton.

Joseph Edwin Barton had succeeded Mr Peacock as Head of Wakefield Grammar School in January 1911 and had therefore known Joseph for a comparatively short period of time. He remained at Wakefield until December 1916 and then moved schools to become the headmaster of Bristol Grammar School the following year. This explains why his condolence letter is sent from Bristol, rather than from Wakefield. Mr Barton remained at Bristol Grammar School until 1938 and in this time became an influential and highly respected figure in the city.

Condolence Letters from Clare College, Cambridge

Joseph's death was reported in the *Wakefield Express* on 19 May 1917 under the heading 'Death of a Wakefield Officer.' This local newspaper printed partial extracts from the condolence letters of McArthur, Cock and Barton. It also printed the following extract from the letter of Captain G.M. Beck, who was one of Joseph's tutors at Clare College: 'I am sure that Clare has lost no more promising and no more brilliant a man since the war began.' The *Wakefield Express* also referred to condolence letters being received from Mr W.L. Mollison, the Master of Clare College, and Mr J.R. Wardale, another college tutor. No extracts appear from either of these letters, but a copy of Mr Wardale's letter has survived separately and is transcribed below:

Clare College,
Cambridge.
May 14th, 1917.

Dear Mr Senior,

I cannot tell you how much your news has distressed me.

Your boy was a very dear pupil of mine, and I have so hoped and prayed that he might be spared; many of my pupils have been almost like sons – if I may say so to a Father – and one by one they are giving up their lives for their country.

If you could spare me a photograph of him, I should be so very grateful. He would have done most valuable work with his quiet force of character and his abilities, if it had not been ordained otherwise.

You must indeed be prostrate with grief. Pray God your third son's life may be spared.

Believe me,

Dear Mr Senior,

Yours most sorrowfully,

J.R. Wardale.

1914 group photograph of Clare College, Cambridge (Author's collection)

Above is a group photograph of Clare College, taken in 1914, which shows Joseph standing on the far left. John Reynolds Wardale (tutor) and William Loudon Mollison (*locum tenens* Master) also appear in this photograph, wearing their mortar boards. The bespectacled Wardale is seated on the left, with the bearded Mollison seated on the right. Wardale lived from 1859 to 1931 and was a Fellow of Clare College from 1882 until his death. He was an eminent classicist and prolific writer, publishing several books on the history of the college. Mollison lived from 1851 to 1929 and was Master of Clare College from 1915 to 1929. Prior to this, he had served as *locum tenens* Master from 1913 to 1915.

Wakefield Grammar School's Obituary

Wakefield Grammar School printed the following obituary to Joseph, which was reproduced in the 1921 commemorative pamphlet that accompanied the unveiling of the school's war memorial:

JOSEPH SENIOR, B.A. – 1903-11. – Lieutenant, Royal Flying Corps and West Yorkshire Regiment, died from wounds received in action on May 9th.

Many Old Savilians will mourn the loss of a brilliant friend, scholar, and athlete, in Joseph Senior. Our school is indeed proud of him, and no one was more devoted to, or had done more for, the honour of Wakefield Grammar School. It is characteristic of the boy that he should have evoked the admiration of all his fellow officers for his amazing courage in action. At a great height he and a fellow officer were heavily attacked by enemy aeroplanes. Senior, notwithstanding the fact that he had had a finger shot off and had received the wound in the stomach which was, alas, to prove fatal, kept working his gun to the very last. Even when lifted out of the machine and taken to the hospital, he had a smile for those around him. His captain says of him "Many times I have attributed my safe keeping to his inexhaustible courage and skill, and then yesterday, but for his extraordinary pluck, we should have probably been shot down." Again he says, "He was the most perfect gentleman one could meet. Amazing calmness and courage on all occasions, combined with perfect manners and such a delightful disposition."

Can we add more to this testimony from men who are facing death every hour of the day, and who know what courage and a high sense of duty can accomplish?

Chapter Five
Lapse of Time

On 6 June 1917 – less than a month after Joseph's death – the War Office sent a letter to Arthur. The letter was to inform him that no further news had been received concerning Walter, reported missing on 3 September the previous year. A similarly worded letter was sent to Charles Mitchell, the father of Second Lieutenant Charles Henry Mitchell, also reported missing that day. It is to be noted that 4 September is the date wrongly quoted by the War Office in both these letters – a mistake that is replicated in further correspondence, but eventually corrected. The following letter is addressed to A. Senior, Esq., Manygates Park, Sandal, Wakefield:

9/14/1531. (C.2. Casualties).   6 June 1917.

Sir,

I am directed to inform you that it is regretted that no further report has been received concerning Second Lieutenant W.T. Senior, 6th Battalion West Yorkshire Regiment, reported Missing 4th September, 1916.

It is regretted that it will consequently be necessary for the Army Council to consider whether they must not now conclude that this officer is dead.

Before this course is taken, however, I am to ask if you will be good enough to confirm the fact that no further news of him has reached you.

I am to add that the official action taken as a result of the decision would consist in the winding up of the officer's accounts, and the removal of his name from the Army List. His name would not appear again in the official casualty lists.

I am,

Sir,

Your obedient Servant,

(Signed) C.F.W.[32]

Arthur's reply to this letter (apparently dated 7 June) has not survived, but its content may be inferred from the reply it prompted from the War Office on 12 June 1917:

Sir,

In reply to your letter of 7th June, 1917, concerning Second Lieutenant W.T. Senior, 6th Battalion, West Yorkshire Regiment, I am directed to inform you that the Army Council have no desire to proceed to the official acceptance of an Officers death on the grounds of lapse of time contrary to the wishes of his relatives. I am therefore to ask whether it is your wish that further action in the matter should be postponed.

At the same time I am to say that the Council consider it only right to inform you that so far as the evidence in their possession goes, there is unfortunately no ground for believing that an Officer could be a prisoner of war for so long a time without news of him being received.

They regret therefore that they are not in a position to hold out any hope that Second Lieutenant Senior is alive.

A leaflet is enclosed showing the steps taken to trace missing officers and men.

It is clear from this letter that Arthur was unwilling to accept Walter's death on the grounds of 'lapse of time'. It is also clear that he firmly believed his son was being kept by the Germans as a prisoner of war. A surviving letter indicates that this was also the belief of Charles Mitchell, who wrote to the War Office on 10 June:

---

32 All correspondence in this chapter between Arthur and the War Office is extracted from TNA WO 374/61338. This also applies to Army Form B.2090a.

148 Chapeltown Road,
Leeds
10/6/17

C.2. Casualties. 9/14/1529
2nd Lieut. C.H. Mitchell,
1/6th West Yorks,
Missing 3rd Septr 1916.

Sir,

In reply to your letter of the 6th June, I beg to state that I have had no definite report from or about my son. Every possible means have been resorted to, Red Cross, Q.V. Jubilee Asscn, the King of Spain, a direct letter to Germany, etc.

We have had several accounts from officers and men engaged on that day, and are led to continue to hope by the following considerations:-

a.   The enemy was not using H.E. shells, our men being mixed up in the German trenches.

b.   An airman is said to have seen a No. of officers taken away prisoners.

c.   The enemy counter attack was in overwhelming numbers, and this it is thought would incline them to take prisoners.

d.   The German report of that day claimed 500 prisoners, and these must be somewhere.

e.   A lady in the Red Cross heard that there was a rumour that the prisoners were taken to Turkey.

f.   Within 14 days our men had all that ground – Beaumont Hamel – and no trace was found of the 5 officers, 3 of the 6th West, and 2 of the 8th West, although 3 of the latter Battn were accounted for, presumably their bodies being found.

g.   Many cases have come under our notice where officers and men have been heard of or have escaped after periods up to 2½ yrs. Presumption of death in some cases has caused great trouble.

I need not say we are tortured past everything by the lack of news, and I think something ought to be done on the following lines:-

Some say that the Prussians defended Beaumont Hamel, others that it was Wertemburgers. Each according to various reports are said to be anxious to take as many prisoners as possible.

Now the operations of that day were peculiar in this respect, that our men took all the position with many prisoners some 12 days later, so that the prisoners then taken would know all that happened on the 3rd Septr. Why then should not the Dept which supervises the prisoners make direct and pointed inquiry of these prisoners, no doubt including some high placed officers. I feel sure that our authorities place no obstacle in the way of similar inquiries from the other side. We know that 2nd Lieut Will was taken because he died in a German hospital a few days later.

We would do anything to get news of our only son. We heard today that a soldier's wife in Morley received 5 letters at once from her husband who had been missing about a year.

Yours obediently
Charles Mitchell[33]

Mr Mitchell's letter prompted the following response from the War Office:

C.2. Casualties. 9/14/1529.   17 July 1917.
Sir,

With reference to your letter of 10th June, 1917, concerning Second Lieutenant C.H. Mitchell, 6th Battalion, West Yorkshire Regiment, I am directed to enclose for your information a leaflet showing the steps taken to trace missing officers and men. Lists of missing officers are also circulated in the camps of German prisoners of war in this country. It is regretted that no news has been received from any of the sources mentioned to indicate that this officer is a prisoner of war, and as far as the evidence in the possession of the Army Council goes there is unfortunately no ground for believing that an officer could be a prisoner of war for

---

33 All correspondence in this chapter between Mr Mitchell and the War Office is extracted from TNA WO 374/48096.

so long a period without news of him being received.

As regards some of the questions raised by you, I am to observe as follows:-

There is so far as is known no foundation for the suggestion that any prisoners of war captured in France have been sent to Turkey; and it is regarded as most improbable that any such action should be taken by the Germans.

No further news has been received of any of the three officers of the 6th Battalion, West Yorkshire Regiment, or two officers of the 8th Battalion, West Yorkshire Regiment, referred to by you, since they were reported as missing. In each case it has been found necessary to consider whether in view of the lapse of time their deaths must not be accepted.

No authenticated case has come under the notice of the Army Council in which an officer, after being missing for so long a period, has been found to be a prisoner of war. The Council would be glad if you would furnish them therefore with the name of the officer in any such cases known to you, in order that further enquiry may be made. They would also be glad to be informed of the name, regimental number and regiment of the soldier whose wife is stated to have received letters from her husband after he had been missing for a year and of any other similar cases as regards soldiers.

I am, Sir, your obedient servant
(signed) C.F.W.

This letter makes indirect reference to Walter and also to Lieutenant Ernest Arthur Turner – the third officer of the 6th Battalion West Yorkshire Regiment to have been reported missing. Turner's death was also presumed to have taken place on 3 September 1916 due to 'lapse of time'. However, unlike Walter and Mitchell, no further news of him was ever received.

The Search of the Battlefield

The British Expeditionary Force was unprepared for the scale of losses it incurred during the Somme Offensive and as a result many of the dead lay unburied where they had fallen for many months after they had been killed.

This had an appalling psychological effect on the survivors, who were forced to endure the sight and smell of former comrades decomposing in no man's land. Continued hostile activity on the part of the enemy did, of course, make their recovery difficult, but even when it was safe to do so the authorities seemed slow to act. This delay no doubt gave false hope to those at home who believed the missing must still be alive. The speed of recovery improved as the war progressed, but relatives often had to endure a long and torturous wait for confirmation of what had happened to their loved ones. The letters of Arthur Senior and Charles Mitchell bear witness to this and were no doubt typical of the letters the War Office received on a regular basis from other parents of missing soldiers and, in Mrs Turner's case, wives of missing husbands. Arthur's letters clearly demonstrate his belief that Walter was still alive, but as the anniversary of his son's disappearance approached, a discovery was made by members of IV Corps:

<u>FIELD SERVICE.</u>   Army Form B.2090a.
Report of Death of an Officer to be forwarded to the War Office
with the least possible delay after receipt of notification of death on
A.F.B.213 or A.F.A.36 or from other official documentary sources.
UNIT.   1/6th WEST YORKSHIRE REGIMENT. T.F.
RANK.   2nd LIEUTENANT.
NAME.   S E N I O R, W.T.
By whom reported. G.O.C. IV Corps, 30/7/17
                         Report of Burials sheet Ref. No.2474.
Date of Death.   3-9-1916.
Place or Hospital.   In the Field, France.
Cause of Death.   Killed in Action.
Place of Burial.   --

STATE WHETHER HE LEAVES A WILL OR NOT.   Not known.
All private documents and effects received from the Front or
Hospital, should be examined, and if any will is found it should be
at once forwarded to the War Office.
Any information received as to verbal expressions by a deceased
Officer of his wishes as to the disposal of his estate should be

reported to the War Office as soon as possible.

P. Hartley Lieutenant, for

Officer i/c Territorial Infantry Northern Section.

Adjutant General's Office at the Base.

Date. 25th August, 1917.

This Army form reveals that the discovery of Walter's body was reported by the General Officer Commanding IV Corps on 30 July, although the form itself is dated 25 August. The men who found his body were evidently part of a burial party, detailed with the grim task of clearing the battlefield of dead soldiers. Arthur received confirmation of Walter's death in a letter dated 3 September 1917 – exactly one year after his son had been reported missing. This letter has not survived, but is referred to in the letter that Arthur sent to the War Office a few days later:

5th September 1917.

Ref 21/11535.

Dear Sir,

<u>2nd Lieut Walter Talbot Senior.</u>

<u>6th West Yorks Regt.</u>

<u>Reported missing at Thiepval, 3rd Sept. 1916.</u>

I have your reply dated 3rd September 1917 to my letter of the 15th August 1917 asking for further information respecting my son.

I was advised by the Record's Office at York that my son was "<u>missing &c</u>" in <u>September 1916</u> and no further <u>Official</u> news reached me until June <u>1917</u> when the War Office 9/14/1531 (C.2. Casualties) advised me that no further report had been received and in view of the lapse of time it was "<u>presumed</u>" that my son died on or since 3rd September 1916.

What I want to know is, upon what evidence it is now determined that my son has been buried, and I also desire to have some personal belonging sent to me to convince me.

My son would have on his person personal belongings and also £10 in money (note case), Ring, Watch, &c &c, and surely if his body has now been found some of his property would be also found and should be sent on to me as evidence.

I trust to have your further reply in due course.
Yours faithfully, [Arthur Senior]

There is no surviving record as to whether Arthur ever received Walter's note case, ring or watch, but it seems unlikely – the looting of corpses on the battlefield is well documented.[34] There is also no record of how Walter's remains were positively identified. There is, however, one other surviving letter which was sent concerning Walter; and, although it fails to shed any more light on the matter, it does at least give some indication of the content of the missing letter sent to Arthur on 3 September:

C.2.Casualties. 9/14/1531.   10 September 1917.
    Sir,

I am directed to inform you that Second Lieutenant W.T. Senior, 6th Battalion, The West Yorkshire Regiment, is now reported as Killed in Action on 3rd September, 1916, on the report of burial party working in France.

This report, it will be seen, definitely confirms the conclusion to which the Army Council had already come as notified to you in the letter *June 18 1917*.

I am again to express their sympathy with you and to say that should you so desire the officer's name can now be inserted in the official casualty lists. I am to ask you to be good enough to communicate your wishes in this respect.

A leaflet relating to the registration and care of graves is enclosed.

I am,
    Sir,
Your obedient Servant,

(Signed) C.F. WATHERSTON

---

34 'A peculiar callousness to the dead came over everybody. Their bodies were rifled for useful parts of equipment, matches and cigarettes' (Tempest, 'History of the Sixth Battalion', p.33). This was true of soldiers on both sides.

Exactly one week after sending Arthur the above letter, the War Office sent the following letter to Mr Mitchell:

C.2. Casualties. 9/14/1529.   17 September, 1917.

Sir,

With reference to the letter from this office of the 17th July, I am directed to inform you with regret that the following report from the Base has now been received concerning Second Lieutenant C.H. Mitchell, 6th Battalion, West Yorkshire Regiment:- "Killed in Action 3rd September, 1916, burial reported by General Officer Commanding 6th Corps, dated 3rd September, 1917."

I am to express the sympathy of the Army Council with you in your bereavement and to add that publication will be made in an early casualty List.

A leaflet relating to the Registration and care of graves is enclosed.

I am, Sir, Your obedient Servant.
(s'd) Herbert Rolfe

It is to be noted that Mitchell's death was reported by the General Officer Commanding 6th Corps, in contrast to Walter's death which was reported by the GOC 4th Corps. Assuming the base reporter has not confused 'IV' with 'VI', this would tend to suggest that there were burial parties from different Army units scouring the same area of land. Mr Mitchell's response to this letter reads as follows:

148 Chapeltown Road, LEEDS
20th Septr 1917.

Dear Sir,

C.2. Casualties. 9/14/1529

2nd Lieut C.H. Mitchell, 6th West Yorks.

I beg to acknowledge your letter of the 17th inst conveying the sad news from the o/c 6th Corps, 3rd Septr 17 that my dear son is buried.

Please obtain for me some more definite particulars so that there

may be no room for doubt; and in order that I may take out Letters
of Administration, etc.

1.   Date he was found. Was his disc on him?
2.   Where buried.
3.   Particulars of effects found on him; he would
       certainly have chequebook, pocketbook, various
       letters and other personal things. These ought to
       be sent to me.

                    Yours faithfully,
                    Charles Mitchell

This letter is remarkably similar to the one that Arthur sent upon receiving
confirmation of his son's death, both letters requesting firm evidence of
identification. Mr Mitchell received a reply to his letter in November, informing
him that his son 'was buried N.N.W. of Albert but the date is not known at
present.' A separate War Office minute sheet indicates that the burial report was
actually received on 20 August. One further letter, sent to Mr Mitchell in April
1918, addresses what is perhaps the most pressing question of all, i.e. how his
son's body was identified:

                                        20 April, 1918.

Sir,

    I am directed to acquaint you that Messrs. Cox & Co's. Shipping
Agency, Ltd., 16 Charing Cross, S.W.1, have been instructed to
forward to you the identity disc of the late Second Lieutenant C.H.
Mitchell, West Yorkshire Regiment. It was stated by the Military
Authorities in France, when returning the disc to this country, that
it was taken from the late Officer's body, and that no other effects
were recovered.

        I am,

            Sir,

                    Your obedient Servant,
                    (sd) L. Miles
                    for the Assistant Financial Secretary.

It need hardly be stated that a body left out in the open would have been in the advanced stages of decomposition a year after death. Likewise exposed letters and pocketbooks would have been reduced to illegible pulp. It is therefore unsurprising that Mitchell's identity disc was the only item that could be salvaged from his remains. Was Walter's identity disc also found on *his* body? There are no surviving documents which can confirm this – and no disc has been handed down through the family – but it does seem likely. Without a disc, positive identification would have proved extremely difficult. Clues might be found in regimental buttons or the stripes on the sleeve of a jacket, but this alone would often prove insufficient – especially if other soldiers of the same regiment or rank were also unaccounted for. Intact paybooks were another known method of identifying the dead, but again only if they could be retrieved in a legible state. The only guaranteed method was to find a man's name engraved in some non-perishable item. That so many men remained unidentified is evidenced by the numerous graves of the Somme which bear only partial descriptions of their occupants. Sometimes only their regiment. Sometimes not even that.

WALTER'S GRAVE

There is no surviving documentation to indicate where on the battlefield Walter's body was found. Nor is there any for Mitchell. Nevertheless, documentation does exist, via the CWGC, to reveal where both men were originally buried. This information is contained within the exhumation reports which were compiled after the Armistice, when both men were relocated to new (more easily maintainable) cemeteries. Walter was originally buried at grid reference 57D.R.19.a.5.4., which was the location of the no longer existing Divion Road Cemetery No.2. It is interesting to compare this with Mitchell, who was originally buried at grid reference 57D.R.19.c.4.5. in another cemetery (of unknown name) which also no longer exists. The fact that the two men were buried in different cemeteries to one another may be due to the fact that their bodies were discovered by burial parties from different Army units. This, in turn, may indicate that they were discovered in different sectors of the battlefield. If this is the case, then it raises the question of just how close to one another they were when they died: the 'spectator' who saw two men caught on the wire may have been witnessing two other men and not Walter and Mitchell after all (see Mr Mitchell's letter to Arthur, quoted in chapter three).

Both men's original grave locations are reproduced on the map below. The 'W' indicates the approximate location of Walter and the 'M' indicates that of Mitchell. Mitchell's burial was about 250 yards east of point 16 of 'The Triangle' – level, but on the wrong side of 'The Pope's Nose'. This seems reasonably close to where he is likely to have been killed. Walter, on the other hand, was buried about 500 yards north of here – way behind the German front-line trench system. It is difficult to know how much significance can be attached to the relative positions of these original burials, but it would certainly have tied up loose ends if both men had been buried in the same cemetery. If Walter's original burial location is an indication that he died to the north of the German front-line trench – and this is pure speculation – then it would open up the possibility that he was recaptured by the Germans during their counter-attack and later died in their custody. This does, however, seem unlikely. The simpler explanation is that his body was carried further to be buried (and in a different direction) for logistical reasons.[35]

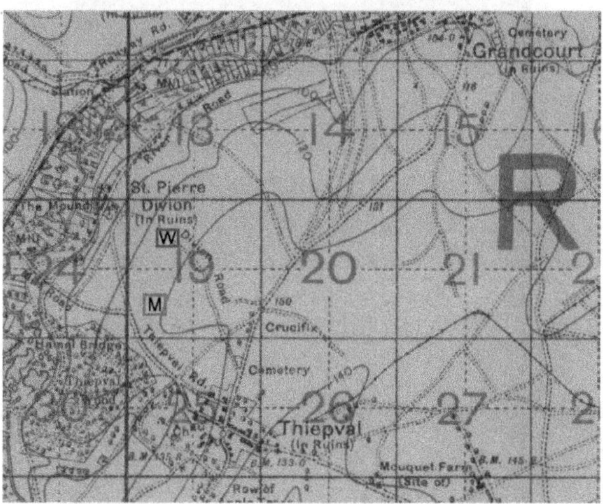

---

35 'The History of the Sixth Battalion' reports the timing of Walter's death with some certainty: 'Lieut. Hearne (A Coy.) reported seeing Lieut. Senior with several men busily bombing German dug-outs, but Senior was killed a few minutes later.' (Tempest, 'History of the Sixth Battalion', p.119). If this account is to be believed, then it would tend to suggest that Walter was killed in the German front-line trench system. However, it is my belief that Tempest (writing in 1921) has made this assumption blindly, since no such certainty exists in any of the first-hand accounts written at the time of Walter's disappearance.

After the Armistice, Walter's body was exhumed and reburied at Connaught Cemetery, on the edge of Thiepval Wood. Mitchell was reburied at Mill Road Cemetery, a short distance from his original burial site. Below is the earliest known photograph of Walter's grave at Connaught Cemetery, which was issued by the Director-General of Graves Registration and sent to Arthur. Such photographs were commonly issued to next of kin with a card indicating the grave position and location of the nearest railway station.

Walter's original grave marker (Author's collection)

As can be seen, infantry grave markers were simple wooden crosses with two narrow metal strips nailed horizontally. The smaller metal strip at the topmost part of the cross bore the initials 'G.R.U.' This stood for 'Grave Registration Unit'. The longer metal strip was embossed with the soldier's rank, surname and regiment. Although attached to the 6th Battalion, 2/LT Senior is recorded as belonging to '3/5 W. Yorks'.

There is only one surviving condolence letter relating to Walter's death. This letter is dated 31 July 1917, which is the day after Walter's body was reported found. It seems extremely unlikely that the palace could have been informed of the discovery of Walter's body by this date. It therefore follows that this letter was sent on presumption of death, based on 'lapse of time', rather than definite confirmation:

Envelope addressed to A. Senior, Esq., Manygates Park, Sandal, Wakefield; date-stamped '1 AUG 17' and red-embossed with the official seal of the Privy Purse Office of Buckingham Palace.

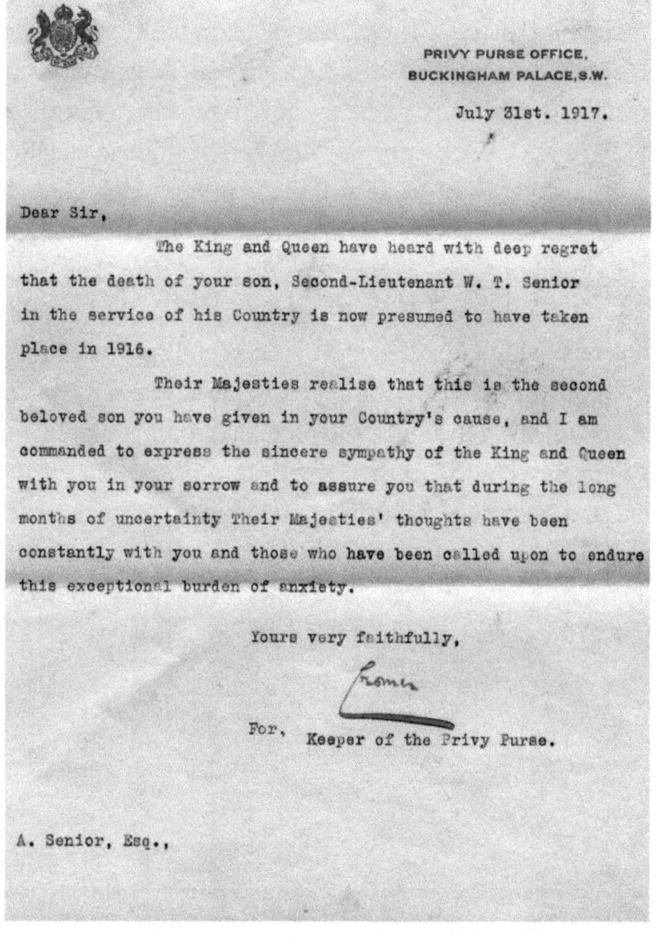

PRIVY PURSE OFFICE,
BUCKINGHAM PALACE, S.W.

July 31st. 1917.

Dear Sir,

The King and Queen have heard with deep regret that the death of your son, Second-Lieutenant W. T. Senior in the service of his Country is now presumed to have taken place in 1916.

Their Majesties realise that this is the second beloved son you have given in your Country's cause, and I am commanded to express the sincere sympathy of the King and Queen with you in your sorrow and to assure you that during the long months of uncertainty Their Majesties' thoughts have been constantly with you and those who have been called upon to endure this exceptional burden of anxiety.

Yours very faithfully,

For, Keeper of the Privy Purse.

A. Senior, Esq.,

Buckingham Palace condolence letter (Author's collection)

Wakefield Grammar School's Obituary

Wakefield Grammar School printed the following obituary to Walter, which was reproduced in the 1921 commemorative pamphlet that accompanied the unveiling of the school's war memorial:

WALTER TALBOT SENIOR. – 1906-1910. – Second-Lieutenant, West Yorkshire Regiment. Reported by the War Office, 11th September, 1917, was killed on September 3rd, 1916.

For just a year we have hoped that Walter Senior might be a prisoner of war, and that the worst might not have happened to him. On September 11th, 1916, the following news came from his Commanding Officer:- "He was last seen in the German trenches, and as at that time, so far as we can ascertain, he was un-wounded, the surmise is that he is probably now a prisoner of war." Again another writes:- "A spectator saw him and two others caught in the wire.[36] The slightest obstacle would keep them long enough, and they would have no choice but to surrender. They did well, and we must be proud of them. None could do more than they did. They used up all bombs, and were using German bombs." Such is the account received, and we can only be proud of Walter Senior, a worthy brother to his elder brother Joseph. It is a sad coincidence that his chum, Walter Smith, should appear in this number among those who have fallen in the war. Both worthy sons of the Old School, and both destined to bring honour to it, however long or short a time they were fated to live. The memory of them will long remain with us, and we hope most sincerely that this may be some comfort to the parents of these fine lads.

---

36 Walter's obituary demonstrates how the removal of a sentence from its original context can alter its meaning: The 'him' that the spectator saw was Hearn, not Walter; it is possible, but not certain, that the other two were Walter and Mitchell. The difference in meaning is subtle, but potentially significant.

Chapter Six
Demobilisation

With Joseph's death on 9 May 1917, George became the last of the three brothers left alive, although confirmation of this fact did not reach him until September 1917, when Walter's status changed from 'missing in action' to 'killed in action'. At the time of Joseph's death, George was a second lieutenant in the 4th Battalion KOYLI, attached to the 2/6 Sherwood Foresters in France. This is known from Arthur's letter to the War Office, dated 11 May 1917, and also from the newspaper article that appeared in the *Wakefield Express* on 19 May 1917. This newspaper article reported that George was 'taking part in the present severe fighting' and printed an extract from a letter sent by George to his father upon hearing the sad news. It read as follows: 'Try to bear up, father. The trees here are speaking to us. Although maimed, cut down, they are trying to carry on, giving forth bud and blossom, teaching us however we are battered, to carry on.'

George had received notification of Joseph's death whilst in divisional reserve at Hancourt, which was about 24 miles south-east of Thiepval. His location here gives some indication of how far the British front line had moved in this sector since the Somme Offensive the previous year. The 2/6 Sherwood Foresters had been involved in heavy fighting on 31 March 1917, when they had successfully captured Jeancourt. A more recent battle had occurred on 29 April. The war diary entry for this date is reproduced below:

2/6 Sherwood Foresters war diary entry – 29 April 1917

Battalion marched to HARGICOURT ROAD from L.11.b.0.5 to L.11.b.5.0 to deploy prior to an attack on QUARRIES and COLOGNE FARM (L.6.c.4.6). The attack was launched at 3.55

am and the QUARRIES were successfully captured and a line
was consolidated EAST of the QUARRIES from L.5.d.9.5 to
L.11.b.9.9. Seven prisoners and 1 Machine Gun were captured[37]

Throughout May and early June, George moved slowly northwards with the
battalion – a period which saw no further battles and was characterised mainly
by the digging and wiring of trenches. On 11 June, the battalion marched into a
camp at Équancourt, where it was to remain in divisional reserve for a further
10 days.

On 17 June, George left the Sherwood Foresters and assumed duties with
the Prisoners of War Company, where he was to stay until demobilisation. There
is a family legend which states that George was moved away from front-line
duties as a direct result of both his brothers being killed in action. This legend
states that a letter was sent by his stepmother, containing words to the effect:
'I've lost two sons in this war and don't want to lose another one.' There is no
hard evidence to support this legend, since no copy of the alleged letter has
survived. Nevertheless, this legend cannot be dismissed completely out of hand.
It is certainly a fact that George was transferred in the month following Joseph's
death and, although Walter's death had not yet been confirmed at this time, the
War Office *had* accepted his probable death on the grounds of 'lapse of time'.
There was no official policy of protecting a soldier if his brothers had been
killed in action and this makes it difficult to assess how seriously a mother's
plea might have been treated in such a circumstance. However, if such a letter
had landed on the desk of a sympathetic commanding officer, it is just possible
that he may have transferred George to a safer position – provided a suitable
vacancy existed.

When balancing up the likelihood of the above, it is worth noting that by
1 June the fighting strength of the 2/6 Sherwood Foresters had increased to 20
officers and 473 other ranks – a much healthier ratio of officers to men than
had existed on 1 May, when it had stood at 14 to 392. The loss of one officer at
this time could therefore be more easily accommodated. Furthermore, George's
transfer took place at a time when the battalion was taking a well-earned rest
behind the lines. This lull in proceedings – a time when 'amusements were

---

37 Extracted from TNA WO 95/3025/4.

provided for the men' – may well have offered a convenient time for such a transfer to take place. Whether it really was a case of *post hoc ergo propter hoc* or a happy coincidence may never be known, but few could dispute the fact that George had 'done his bit' and deserved a break from the action.[38]

Details relating to George's time with the Prisoners of War Company are sketchy. There is a surviving Army record which indicates that he joined No.29 Prisoner of War Company on 28 June 1917.[39] However the location of his camp is not named and it is unclear how long he stayed here. Family legend has it that George spent some time based on the Isle of Wight – if this is correct, then No.29 POW Company may well have been based on this island. Later clues as to George's whereabouts come from papers found amongst his personal effects. The first of these clues is an invoice made out to 'Lt. G. Senior' and addressed to 'P of W Camp, Blandford, Dorset'. This invoice is dated 27 September 1918 and was issued by Will. R. Rose of 133 & 134 High Street in Oxford. 'Wilrose' was a photography shop in Oxford and George evidently sent an undeveloped roll of film to be developed here, whilst he was stationed at Blandford. The developed prints were retained by George in their original 'Wilrose' pouch, which helps to date them and also positively connects them to this particular prisoner of war camp. The subject matter of these photographs suggests a fairly relaxed atmosphere existed at Blandford: in one photograph George is standing poised with a golf club in mid-swing; in another he is seated on the grass cradling two small dogs in his arms. These dogs were quite possibly used as ratters to keep vermin under control. It is known that George brought a Jack Russell back with him after he left the Army and gave it to his father as a present. This dog was apparently named 'Toby' and could do tricks. Toby appears in a family album standing on his hind legs and bears a striking resemblance to the dog shown here under George's right arm.

---

38 On 21 June, shortly after George had left the 2/6 Sherwood Foresters, the battalion resumed front-line
   duties and between this date and 30 June suffered 13 casualties. This is recorded in the battalion war
   diary, which lists the casualties as nine men wounded and four killed. One of the dead was a second
   lieutenant – had George remained in this battalion, it could quite easily have been him.

39 This information is recorded on an Army Form B.103 (usually used to record casualties) and is located
   within TNA WO 374/61329.

George at Blandford Prisoner of War Camp, playing golf and cradling two dogs in his arms
(Author's collection)

Blandford Prisoner of War Camp was located on the eastern side of Blandford Naval Camp, close to the village of Tarrant Monkton. As with all such camps, it was visited by the Swiss Legation in order to assess the welfare of the prisoners. The first Swiss report was compiled in March 1917 and revealed that there were 1,395 prisoners at the camp at this time; and that there had been 20 attempted escapes in the previous 12 months. Many of the prisoners were employed in skilled and semi-skilled work that covered everything from motor repairs and plumbing to agricultural labouring and work in sawmills.

Photographs of German prisoners of war detained at Blandford Camp in 1917 are to be found within the King's College Archive Centre of the University of Cambridge.[40] These photographs depict men digging with pickaxes and spades; men wheeling wooden wheelbarrows in convoy between steep banks of earth; and men carrying sawn wood from felled trees, smoke rising from bonfires in the background. Other photographs depict prisoners relaxing in their leisure time. Track and field events, such as baton racing and the high

---

40 These photographs are to be found within AEF/4/11, amongst various other documents.

jump, appear in this latter category – as do football matches. Another batch of photographs is kept within the archives of the Royal Signals Museum in Dorset, which occupies roughly the same site as the former POW camp (the POW camp having been a little further to the east). Standing out amongst their collection is a picture of 'Fritz', balancing a plank on his shoulder and carrying a hammer. This particular photograph comes from the album of Lieutenant J. Victor Yates of the RAF and dates to circa May 1918. The RAF moved into the Naval Camp at around this time and eventually took over the huts occupied by the prisoners of war, forcing them to go under canvas nearby.[41]

'Fritz' at Blandford Prisoner of War Camp (Image © Royal Signals Museum)

George was promoted to lieutenant on 19 June 1918, almost exactly a year after joining the Prisoners of War Company. His promotion was publicised in the *Yorkshire Post* on 6 July, prompting his father to send him a congratulatory note. George posed for two photographs after he became a lieutenant, both of

---

41 Blandford Camp was dismantled in 1920, enjoyed a brief spell as a motor racing track, and is today
   (2019) the home of the Royal Corps of Signals.

which appear to have been taken by someone with the surname of 'Bacon' at a photography studio in Leeds. Miraculously George's jacket – the actual one he was wearing in these photographs – has survived. Apart from some moth damage, it is otherwise in remarkably good condition. The jacket is pictured below, alongside George's photograph. The three blue chevrons on the lower right sleeve are an indication that George had completed three years of overseas service. The red-white-blue ribbon bar above his left breast pocket is an indication that he had been awarded his 1914-1915 Star – the first of three medals he would eventually receive, the other two being the Victory Medal and the British War Medal. (George's brothers would be awarded their medals posthumously, along with memorial plaques bearing their names.)

George in KOYLI uniform, photographed shortly after being promoted to lieutenant (Author's collection)

George's surviving KOYLI uniform jacket (Author's collection)

The Armistice of 11 November 1918 signalled the end of the Great War. However, the full demobilisation of the Army took longer and George was still serving at Blandford in March 1919. At the end of this month, the Swiss Legation returned in order to compile another report. This report bears testimony to the fact that German prisoners were still being detained here, despite almost five months having elapsed since the end of hostilities. Their continued detention puzzled many. In April 1919, a petition for release was signed by 2,300 German prisoners of war at Brocton Camp in Staffordshire, which asked the not unreasonable question: '*Unter welchen Voraussetzungen werden wir nun zurückbehalten?*'[42]

---

42 This petition is to be found within TNA FO 383/506.

Whatever the reasons for their continued detention, the prisoners were generally well looked after in most camps. There were certainly no complaints reported at Blandford. The men here were provided with adequate facilities and enjoyed a varied diet which included bread, biscuits, pork, horseflesh, bacon, fish, coffee, tea, potatoes, peas, beans, rice, oatmeal, margarine, cocoa, maize and smoked or pickled herrings. Three deaths had occurred in the previous autumn, but these had been as a result of the prevailing influenza pandemic. The Swiss report revealed that there were 210 German military prisoners kept at Blandford in March 1919, a reduction that was mainly caused by large numbers being transferred to Dorchester. Approximately one-third of the remaining prisoners were employed in aircraft construction and another third in farm work.

Toby the dog, who was 'demobilised' along with George and given to his father as a present
(Gent family collection)

On 14 March 1919, George was sent correspondence from the University of Oxford, following an enquiry he had made to the School of Agriculture and Forestry. He was evidently making plans for his life after the war and had written to Professor Somerville, requesting a syllabus for the course he was hoping to pursue there. George clearly felt an affinity with Oxford and this may have been partly due to his military training there and also perhaps due to it being the home of his kindly ex-headmaster, Mr Matthew Peacock. Confirmation of his disembodiment was transmitted to George by the War Office in a typed letter dated 21 July 1919. This letter was addressed to Manygates Park, his family home in Wakefield. Italics indicate the manual insertion of writing in the blank spaces between the typed print – an indication that this was a standard template issued to all disembodied soldiers:

> Sir,
>
> I am commanded by the Army Council to inform you that in consequence of the demobilisation of the Army you have been disembodied as from the *10.7.19* inclusive.
>
> You will receive a further notification of any gratuity to which you may be entitled.
>
> You should report any change of permanent address to the:-
> *Secretary War Office S.W.1.*
>
> I am also to take this opportunity of conveying the thanks of the Army Council for your services to the Country during the late war, and for the excellent work you have done.

For George the war was finally over and, although he had been contemplating a move to Oxford, he returned instead to the University of Leeds. George had studied at Leeds, prior to enlistment, on a two-year agricultural course which he had begun in 1912. From 1919 to 1922 he returned for a three-year agricultural course, holding one of the agricultural scholarships of the Ministry of Agriculture & Fisheries for ex-officers. As well as studying for this course, he also played rugby for the university and was vice-captain of the team that won the Whitworth Challenge Shield in the 1921-22 season. The captain of this team was Roger Sayce and it was through Roger that George was introduced to his future wife, Constance Gibbings. Con was Roger's sister-in-law and the pair met when George visited Roger's house and found her babysitting Roger junior. He would later marry Con in 1924 in Liverpool, the bride's family home.

George shaking hands with University of Leeds teddy bear rugby mascot (Author's collection)

George graduated from Leeds in 1922 with a BSc in Agriculture and then remained at the university as a temporary assistant in his old department. In 1923 he moved to the south-west of England and became an agricultural lecturer for Wiltshire County Council, working under Robert Boutflour. The following year he bought a farm near Bristol and, five years later, became Secretary of the Bristol Area Milk Committee. The appointment of this 'able young farmer' was publicised in the *Evening World* on 11 October 1929, in an article which warned he would have his work cut out as 'there is a great deal of unrest in the milk world at present'. In an unrelated article the same newspaper reported that 'telegrams are going out of fashion… the telephone, on the other hand, has come into its own'.

George loading hay onto a cart with Jack Senior, his first cousin once removed, circa 1929
(Author's collection)

George became a father in 1929 with the birth of Miriam, whose birth was followed by that of Joseph in 1931 and finally Mary in 1934. George had named Joseph in memory of his late eldest brother, but having done so it seems he found it too painful to speak Joe's name. Consequently his son became known by his middle name of Talbot, which had also been Walter's middle name. Shortly before Mary's birth, the family left their farm (leaving cousin Jack in charge) and moved to an address in Great Thurlow, West Sussex. Here George acted as land agent for the Thurlow Estate, which at that time was owned by Charles Foster Ryder. The family lived in a large house at Thurlow, situated next to an orchard. A corner of this orchard soon became the final resting place for a cache of treasured Great War mementos – George had brought these back from the Western Front, but Con was unhappy about having them in the house and so insisted that he got rid of them. Exactly what was buried is unclear, but the cache may have included a German Mauser pistol.

A snapshot of life in Thurlow at this time is to be found within the autobiography of Sue Ryder, the renowned charity worker. Sue was the daughter of Charles Ryder and in adult life became the founder of the 'Sue Ryder Foundation for the sick and disabled', work which earned her an OBE. In the early chapters of her autobiography, Sue describes the close-knit community of Thurlow – along with some of its more memorable characters:

> Many individuals living and working around us had been involved in the fighting… Several had been affected by the gas attacks on the Western Front from April 1915 onwards. A figure I remember used to bicycle regularly along the local roads, swearing at anybody who passed – he had been shell-shocked and was disturbed, with no other occupation than bicycling on through the four seasons of the year.[43]

The outbreak of World War Two was announced to the congregation of Great Thurlow Church on the morning of Sunday 3 September 1939. Soon the village became home to evacuees from London and, after the Dunkirk evacuation, minds turned seriously towards the threat of an imminent German invasion. George's eldest daughter Miriam remembers her father being captain of the Home Guard at this time. Meetings were apparently convened in one of the local pubs, although Miriam was not privy to their activities.

George became the last land agent to work for the Ryder family as the Thurlow Estate was sold following the death of Charles in February 1942. Mr Ryder's death left George without employment and his family was now faced with a brief period of uncertainty. At around this time George's father was also becoming increasingly unwell and displaying symptoms consistent with dementia. Arthur was still living in Yorkshire at this time and being cared for by Margaret, his youngest daughter with second wife Kate (who had died in 1929). He eventually died on 23 March 1944. In the years leading up to his death, he expressed his belief that the Germans would finally release Walter from captivity at the end of the war. It is impossible to know whether he was referring to the 'current war' or whether senility had caused him to regress. One thing beyond doubt is the profound effect Walter's disappearance had on Arthur: he was never fully convinced that his son's body had been found. Three days before Arthur's

---

43 Sue Ryder, *And the Morrow Is Theirs* (Bristol: Sue Ryder Foundation, 1975), p.13.

death, George wrote a letter to his own son, who was in an Oxford hospital at the time and being cared for by Doctor Gathorne Robert Girdlestone. Talbot had just undergone an operation to have his right leg amputated, the final in a long series of operations that had plagued his childhood. His leg had originally been damaged in childbirth and all previous attempts to reset it had failed. In his letter, George gives the following fatherly advice and encouragement:

> My dear Talbot… you will find that life with an artificial limb is not as dreadful as it sounds & on this point I expect Mr Girdlestone will have enlightened you & I won't enlarge any further on this. What we are going to do is to show the world that we can surmount difficulties & still come out smiling on the top. This is what Daddy does when he meets a big set-back – he just grits his teeth, sticks it & makes up his mind to come out triumphant in the end & this is what I want you to do.

Although a deeply personal letter, this extract is reproduced here because it gives some insight into George's character and the grim stoicism that had carried him through the war. 'Gritting his teeth and sticking it' was evidently how he had coped with the death of both his brothers. Moreover, he would certainly have witnessed soldiers with missing limbs returning from the battlefield – men who had adapted to post-war life with wooden prosthetics.

During 1944, George found new employment as the South Devon area agent for the National Trust and subsequently lived with his family in Budlake House on the Killerton Estate near Exeter. During the summer of 1947 he was visited by Roger Sayce junior – the young man who, as a baby, had unwittingly introduced him to Con. Roger was visiting George in order to gain work experience. He recorded this visit many years later in his self-published autobiography, which included the following candid insight:

> [George] was a somewhat forbidding man (I remember, as a small boy, being quite frightened by him) and liable to find his temper stretched beyond his limits. At least so this appeared at home. But at work with his staff and in meeting tenants and other[s] he was

the opposite – quite amenable and pleasant and efficient.[44]

George retired reluctantly in 1956, having reached the 60-year upper age limit imposed by the Trust upon its agents. At his leaving ceremony he was presented with a log chest, made from an oak tree felled on the Killerton Estate 25 years previously. He was also presented with the very latest in modern audio equipment – a mains portable VHF radio set. In a local newspaper article which reported his departure, George was described by his secretary, Mr H.S. Kemble, as 'an individualist in a world which regrettably was becoming filled with people who acted and believed alike.' He retired to Cornwall with Con and spent his final years at 'Carne Vean' in Manaccan, a cottage owned by the National Trust and tenanted to retiring staff. It was here, at 'Carne Vean', that he died on 23 January 1969, at the age of 73. Following his cremation, his ashes were scattered near his home. George is commemorated at the National Trust estate at Cotehele in Cornwall, one of his favourite haunts, where his name is engraved on a memorial bench to the north-east of the upper garden.

---

44 R.B. Sayce, *A Rural Surveyor* (Wantage: R.B. Sayce, 2000), pp.61-62.

George's memorial inscription at Cotehele in Cornwall (photographed with the kind permission of the National Trust)

George's post-war life illustrates all that was denied to his brothers: marriage, children, a log chest upon retirement… The bullets that ended the lives of Joseph and Walter ended also the promise of their younger days. And yet, paradoxically, they remain for ever young: 'Age shall not weary them, nor the years condemn.' As a girl, Miriam can remember Remembrance Sunday was always an especially solemn occasion for her father. Perhaps the anger that sometimes boiled within him was a symptom of the gap left in his life by the loss of his two, dearly missed, brothers.

CHAPTER SEVEN
GREATER LOVE HATH NO MAN

CONNAUGHT CEMETERY

Second Lieutenant Walter Talbot Senior is buried in Connaught Cemetery, on the eastern edge of Thiepval Wood. To the north of this wood is the area of land where he fought and died on 3 September 1916. Nearby, and clearly visible from the cemetery, is the Ulster Tower – an imposing memorial built to commemorate the men of the 36th (Ulster) Division. Connaught Cemetery contains 1,288 graves and Walter is one of only 644 identified casualties. The rest are 'known only unto God'. Walter's headstone is flanked on either side by unidentified servicemen. The headstone to his left reads: 'An Irish soldier of the Great War'. The headstone to his right has an even briefer description: 'A soldier of the Great War'. Walter's inscription reads as follows: 'Second Lieutenant W.T. Senior West Yorkshire Regiment 3rd September 1916 age 22. Greater love hath no man than this'. This biblical epitaph is taken from John 15:13, the full reading of which is 'Greater love hath no man than this, that a man lay down his life for his friends' (King James Bible version). Walter's grave reference is II.K.4.

There are a further nine soldiers of the West Yorkshire Regiment who also died on 3 September 1916 buried in Connaught Cemetery: Private Joseph Greenhow, who served as J. Taylor (3253); Private F. Wharton (201454); Private A.P. Brogden (240732); Lance Corporal Leonard Buckle (2819); Private G.B. Crowe (1693); Private Charles Inman (1476); Private A.A. Smith (241237); Private W. Spinks (2677); and Private J.A. White (1242). Also buried here are 14 soldiers of the Duke of Wellington's Regiment, who had fought on the right flank of the West Yorkshire Regiment the same day.

MILL ROAD CEMETERY

Second Lieutenant Charles Henry Mitchell is buried in Mill Road Cemetery, approximately 500 yards north-east of Connaught Cemetery and accessible via a rising track. This cemetery contains 1,305 graves and Mitchell is one of only 489 identified casualties. Mitchell was reported to have been 'caught in the wire' with Walter as both men were retreating across no man's land. Although it is not known how either of these men died, it seems likely that they were killed by rifle or machine-gun fire as they struggled to free themselves from the barbed wire in which they had reportedly become entangled. The fact that Mitchell is buried here, in a different cemetery to Walter, despite the fact that both men are believed to have been quite close together when they were killed, may be due to the fact that their bodies were discovered by burial parties from different Army units (see chapter five). A surviving note, written by his father on 9 May 1919, suggests that Mitchell had volunteered for military service soon after the outbreak of war. This note reads as follows: 'Never were there finer youths than those who joined in 1914.'[45] Mitchell's inscription reads as follows: 'Second Lieutenant C.H. Mitchell West Yorkshire Regiment 3rd September 1916 Age 25. A glorious life full of love. A noble death saving others. Our only son.' Mitchell's grave reference is XII.D.2.

Also buried in Mill Road Cemetery is Second Lieutenant Thomas Christopher Vause, 8th Battalion West Yorkshire Regiment, who was again reported missing following the 3 September attack. He is indirectly referred to in Mr Mitchell's letter to the War Office, dated 10 June 1917 (see chapter five). The 8th Battalion had been fighting alongside and on the left flank of the 6th Battalion the day of the battle, and Vause was one of two officers from this battalion to be reported missing that day. Vause was aged 33 when he died and his grave reference is XII.B.6.

A further 28 soldiers of the West Yorkshire Regiment and 85 soldiers of the Duke of Wellington's Regiment, who all fought alongside one another on 3 September 1916, are also buried in Mill Road Cemetery.

---

45 This comment was written by Mr Mitchell on a War Office letter informing him that he would be the recipient of a memorial plaque and scroll, dedicated to his son. This letter (Form 1p.) is located within TNA WO 374/48096.

Walter's headstone at Connaught Cemetery, Thiepval (Author's collection)

Mitchell's headstone at Mill Road Cemetery, Thiepval (Mitchell's portrait © IWM HU 125734)

THE SUNKEN ROAD

Connaught Cemetery and Mill Road Cemetery lie on opposite sides of the D73 road to Hamel. This road leads on up towards the Ulster Tower and then forks sharply to the left, straight ahead being a rough track across fields. As the road veers away from the tower, it gradually sinks lower into the landscape and the banks of earth on either side become noticeably higher in comparison. This section of the D73 is the location of 'The Sunken Road', where Walter crossed on 3 September 1916 in order to attack 'The Triangle' to the north – tarmac now covering the original surface. By standing on the southern bank of this road, with your back to Thiepval Wood, you will be standing in the footsteps of the 6th Battalion on the morning of the attack. The relevant section is pictured below, with a poppy marking the southern bank. There are in fact several 'sunken roads' in this part of France, their formation caused by erosion of the light chalky soil that is a characteristic of the region.

'The Sunken Road' at Thiepval

THE TRIANGLE

The capture of 'The Triangle' was the objective of the 6th Battalion on 3 September 1916, but all trace of this trench system has long since disappeared due to ploughing. However, there still remains one visual reminder of the German occupation: leading away northwards from the entrance to the Ulster Tower is a rough track which continues down towards the village of Saint-Pierre-Division. Approximately 120 yards along this track, on the right, is a misshapen lump of concrete surrounded by broken iron girders which poke out of the ground. These are the remnants of a German observation post which was located at 'The Pope's Nose', adjacent to 'The Triangle'. The reinforced concrete was designed to withstand artillery shelling so that the observer could give advance warning of an infantry attack to his fellow soldiers.

This observation post was situated close to point 16 of 'The Triangle'. It is roughly from this point that Walter, Mitchell and Hearn made their final stand against the advancing enemy. And it is from here that all three men made their final dash back across no man's land. Somewhere in this now-peaceful field (roughly between the observation post and the D73 road) is where Walter and Mitchell were reported to have been 'caught in the wire' – and where Hearn 'nearly stopped a shell'. Below is a modern-day aerial view of the battlefield with the historic trench lines of 'The Triangle' overlaid on top. The hash symbol indicates the location of the observation post at 'The Pope's Nose' and the orange arrow indicates the possible route taken back across no man's land by Hearn.

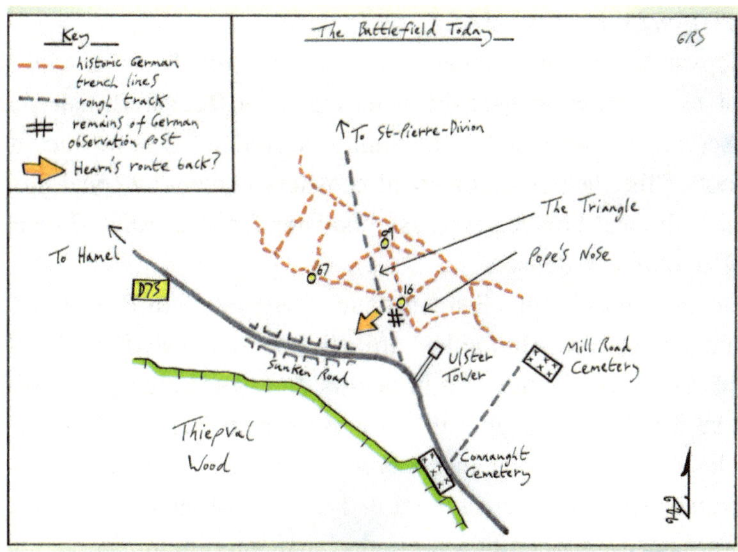

Modern-day aerial view of the battlefield with the historic trench lines of 'The Triangle' overlaid on top

Remains of German observation post at 'The Pope's Nose' with the Ulster Tower in the background (photographed from the west)

THE THIEPVAL MEMORIAL

The Thiepval Memorial is situated on the edge of Thiepval village. This memorial to the missing lists the names of over 72,000 British and South African servicemen who died in the Somme sector and have no known graves. At the foot of the memorial is a small cemetery containing equal numbers of Commonwealth and French graves, symbolising the joint Anglo-French nature of the 1916 Somme Offensive.

Lieutenant Ernest Arthur Turner, Lance Corporal Cyril Pearce and Second Lieutenant John Cecil Bottomley are all commemorated at the Thiepval Memorial. Lieutenant Turner was in the first line of the attack with Walter and was last seen fighting with him in the first German line. His body was never found. The same is true of Lance Corporal Pearce, who had bravely tried to rescue Walter when he was captured early on in the attack. Both Turner and Pearce were aged 33 when they were declared 'missing in action' and it was only subsequently that they were determined to have died on 3 September. Second Lieutenant Bottomley served with the 8th Battalion West Yorkshire Regiment and was the second officer of this regiment to be reported missing on 3 September (see Vause above). Lieutenant Ernest Arthur Turner, Lance Corporal Cyril Pearce and Second Lieutenant John Cecil Bottomley all share the same memorial reference number: Pier and Face 2A 2C and 2D.

Lieutenant Turner's widow, Helen Katharine Mary, spent her entire widowed life not knowing where her husband's body lay. She continued to teach at Harvington School in Ealing and became joint headmistress with a Miss Emerton in 1940. Mrs Turner remained in this post until her retirement in 1956 and the retention of her surname suggests that she did not remarry.[46]

---

46 Lieutenant Turner also had a brother by the name of Chevalier Moore Turner, who does not appear to have fought in the war. His address is recorded on a 'next of kin' form as being in Ferndale, Humboldt County, California (TNA WO 374/69849).

The Thiepval Memorial

Turner's inscription on the Thiepval Memorial

Turner's portrait © IWM HU 119375

CAPTAIN HEARN

Captain Stanley George Hearn fought alongside Walter on 3 September 1916 and made it safely back across no man's land, although he was very nearly killed by an artillery shell as he returned. He went on to survive the Great War. Sadly, two of his brothers were killed: Private Robert Hearn served with the 22nd Battalion Royal Fusiliers and died of wounds on 28 July 1916 during the Battle of Delville Wood, part of the Somme Offensive, aged 30; Second Lieutenant Leonard Hearn served with the 6th Battalion Duke of Cornwall's Light Infantry and was killed in action on 18 October 1917, aged 27, at Sanctuary Wood during the third battle of Ypres. Both brothers are commemorated at St. Saviour's church in Dartmouth, Devon.

After the war, Stanley enjoyed a successful married life and was the father of two daughters. He died at the age of 88 on 9 August 1976, having outlived his wife. His last will and testament includes the following words: 'I have had a good life which has lasted much longer than I at one time expected.'

BAILLEUL COMMUNAL CEMETERY EXTENSION

Lieutenant Joseph Senior is buried in the extension to Bailleul Communal Cemetery in Northern France, close to the Belgian border. This cemetery contains 4,344 identified casualties of the Great War and there are 55 men of the Royal Flying Corps buried here. Joseph's original grave marker had been a propeller cross, as was the norm with airmen at this time, but sometime in the 1920s all propeller crosses were replaced with headstones. The Latin motto of the RFC features prominently at the top of all these headstones and has continued to be the motto of the Royal Air Force today: *per ardua ad astra* ('through adversity to the stars'). Joseph's inscription reads as follows: 'Lieutenant Joseph Senior Royal Flying Corps formerly West Yorkshire Regt 9th May 1917 Age 24. Late classical scholar B.A. Owst prizeman and winner of Dr Green's cup Clare Coll Cambridge.' Joseph's grave reference is III.B.70.

There are three other airmen from No.45 Squadron buried in this cemetery: Captain C.H. Jenkins, who died 22 May 1917; Second Lieutenant James Harold Hartley, who died 22 July 1917; and Lieutenant Robert Leslie Clegg, who died 3 September 1917. Also buried here are 11 airmen from No.20 Squadron, which shared the aerodrome at Sainte-Marie-Cappel with No.45 Squadron from mid-April 1917. No.1 Squadron, based next to Bailleul Asylum, accounts for a further 11 burials. Nos. 42 and 53 Squadrons, based at Bailleul Town Ground Aerodrome, account for 10 more. Also worthy of note are the burials relating to the Royal Air Force. The RAF was formed on 1 April 1918 when the Royal Flying Corps and Royal Naval Air Service amalgamated to form the world's first independent air force and there are two RAF burials in this cemetery: Second Lieutenant Frederick James Church, who died 13 July 1918; and Lieutenant C.S. Johnson, who died 13 August 1918.

BAILLEUL ASYLUM

Following the aerial combat of 9 May 1917, Joseph was treated for gunshot wounds at No.53 Casualty Clearing Station. Despite the best efforts of the medics, it was here that he subsequently died. At this time No.53 C.C.S. was based in Bailleul Asylum, which was on the north-eastern side of Bailleul and adjacent to the aerodrome used by No.1 Squadron. During the war the asylum continued to treat the 'lunatics' in its wards whilst sharing facilities with the British medical units stationed here. The asylum was used by the British until the building was evacuated in April 1918 in anticipation of a second German occupation of the town – the first occupation having taken place in October 1914. Sadly, it was during the subsequent French-British counteroffensive of 1918 that the asylum was completely destroyed. Today a new psychiatric hospital has been built on the site of the old asylum, and this serves as a visual reminder of where Joseph spent his final hours.

Bailleul Psychiatric Hospital (Établissement Public de Santé Mentale des Flandres), located in Bailleul on the Route de Locre

Joseph's headstone at extension to Bailleul Communal Cemetery (Author's collection)

McArthur's headstone at Harlebeke New British Cemetery (Author's collection)

HARLEBEKE NEW BRITISH CEMETERY

Captain Lawrence William McArthur was the last pilot that Joseph flew with, and the two shared at least 36 missions together. McArthur is buried in Harlebeke New British Cemetery in Harelbeke, Belgium.[47] Tragically, he survived Joseph by only 18 days. On the morning of 27 May 1917, he left Sainte-Marie-Cappel on an offensive patrol with seven other aircraft and never returned. Seven hostile aircraft were encountered during this patrol and the squadron record book records the following entry next to McArthur's name: 'Took part in fight and last seen at 12,000 ft. 2 miles over lines. Not yet returned.'[48] McArthur was later reported killed in action along with his observer, Second Lieutenant Allan Stewart Carey. The plane he was flying (A/8226) was the same machine that he had flown on 9 May when Joseph had been fatally wounded. This machine twice suffered from engine problems on the morning of 27 May before finally being able to join the other aircraft. It is not known whether there were further problems with the engine during the aerial combat that followed, but it seems a distinct possibility.

Contemporary German sources indicate that McArthur's plane was downed by *Offizierstellvertreter* (Warrant Officer) Max Müller of Jasta 28 over enemy-held territory near Ypres. McArthur and Carey were buried by the Germans. After the Armistice their graves were relocated, along with many other graves from the surrounding battlefields and cemeteries, to the newly created Harlebeke New British Cemetery. This cemetery is located 20 miles east of Ieper (Ypres) town centre and there are 1,116 Commonwealth servicemen from the Great War buried or commemorated here. McArthur's inscription reads as follows: 'Captain L.W. McArthur MC. Hon. Artillery Company attd. Royal Flying Corps 27th May 1917.' McArthur's grave reference is XVII.B.12.

McArthur's observer, Second Lieutenant Allan Stewart Carey, is buried alongside him. His grave reference is XVII.B.11. Carey had replaced Joseph as McArthur's observer following Joseph's death.

---

47 The name of the cemetery appears to be an inadvertent corruption of the name of the town.
48 Extracted from TNA AIR 1/1787/204/151/4.

THE ARRAS FLYING SERVICES MEMORIAL

Captain William George Bransby Williams is commemorated at the Arras Flying Services Memorial, which is located in the Faubourg-d'Amiens Cemetery in the western part of Arras. This memorial commemorates almost 1,000 airmen of the Royal Naval Air Service, the Royal Flying Corps, the Australian Flying Corps and the Royal Air Force, who were killed on the Western Front and who have no known graves. Williams was killed on 12 May 1917 (three days after Joseph) whilst flying over enemy lines to the east of Arras. He was serving with No.19 Squadron at the time, flying in SPAD VII (B1560), which was a single-seat fighter aircraft. His body was never found. Prior to serving with No.19 Squadron, Williams had flown with No.45 Squadron and whilst here Joseph acted as his observer on 43 separate occasions. Williams was aged 19 at the time of his death. Bizarrely the number 19 also features in his home address – 19 Eton Court, Eton Avenue, London.

The Arras Flying Services Memorial with dedication to Williams (Author's collection)

TOURNAI COMMUNAL CEMETERY, ALLIED EXTENSION

Lieutenant Francis George Truscott is buried in the allied extension to Tournai Communal Cemetery in Belgium, which contains 689 Commonwealth burials of the Great War. Truscott joined No.45 Squadron as an observer at the same time as Joseph and the two had previously served together in the 4th Corps Cyclist Battalion. He is referred to in Joseph's letter to his father, written on Easter Monday 1917 (see chapter four). Truscott's inscription reads as follows: 'Lieutenant Francis G. Truscott MC. Suffolk Regiment and Royal Flying Corps 6th April 1917 age 22. Dearly loved son of Sir George and Lady Truscott. God is here.' Truscott's grave reference is II.J.30.

Also commemorated in this cemetery is Second Lieutenant James Edward Blake, whom Joseph had previously flown with on one occasion during an aborted reconnaissance mission. Blake had originally been buried in Froyennes German Cemetery, but his body could not be located for subsequent exhumation and reburial. He is commemorated with a special memorial headstone, situated at the southern end of the cemetery. Despite the implied date on this memorial, Blake appears to have died as a prisoner of war on 8 April 1917.[49] Blake's inscription reads as follows: 'To the memory of Second Lieutenant J.E. Blake Royal Flying Corps 6th April 1917. Killed in action and buried at the time in Froyennes German Cemetery whose grave is now lost. Their glory shall not be blotted out.'

Truscott and Blake were two of six members of No.45 Squadron to be reported missing over Tournai on 6 April 1917. The remaining four officers are all buried in this cemetery: Lieutenant John Arthur Marshall, aged 19, who was Truscott's pilot (II.J.31); Captain William Stead Brayshay, aged 29, who was Blake's observer (II.J.26); Second Lieutenant Colin St. George Campbell, aged 33, who was Edwards' pilot (II.J.1); and Captain Donald William Edwards MC, aged 26, who was Campbell's observer (II.J.7).

In common with Blake, Brayshay died as a prisoner of war. The precise date of his death is unclear, but his father held onto the hope that he was still alive long after his disappearance. In June 1918, he wrote a letter to the War Office in which

---

49 A letter written to his sister Frances, on 6 January 1920, relates that Blake's death had been accepted for official purposes as having occurred 'whilst a prisoner of war on 8th April 1917 from wounds received in action' (TNA WO 339/59987). This date also appears in a dedication to Blake on his parents' gravestone in Darlington's West Cemetery, close to his family home.

he stated the following: 'I do not intend to take out [administration of my son's estate] until the war is over and all prisoners returned, and if then it is necessary I will then take out letters of administration of his estate.' In an earlier letter, written in August 1917, he had asked the War Office for permission to come to Tournai to look for his son: 'I hope the Germans shortly will be driven beyond this district. I ask you when this occurs for you to give me permission to go there to find out. He may or may not be dead and I want more evidence than you have got.'[50]

The following letter was written in August 1918 and addressed to the wife of Captain Edwards:

> The Secretary of the War Office presents his compliments to Mrs C.G.K. Edwards, and begs to inform her that included in a consignment of effects of deceased British Officers returned to this country by the German Government was a ring bearing the name of the late Captain D.W. Edwards, Army Service Corps and Royal Flying Corps.
>
> It is regretted that no information is forthcoming regarding the circumstances of its recovery.
>
> The ring is being forwarded to Mrs Edwards under separate registered cover.[51]

---

50 Both these letters are to be found within TNA WO 374/8721.

51 This letter is to be found in TNA WO 339/22819.

Truscott's headstone at Tournai Communal Cemetery, Allied Extension (Author's collection)

Blake's memorial headstone at Tournai Communal Cemetery, Allied Extension (Author's collection)

LONGUENESSE (SAINT-OMER) SOUVENIR CEMETERY

Second Lieutenant Henry Griffith Pagan Lowe is buried in Longuenesse Souvenir Cemetery, which is in Northern France on the southern outskirts of Saint-Omer. This cemetery contains 2,874 Commonwealth burials of the Great War. Lowe was the first pilot that Joseph flew with, although they shared an aircraft on only two occasions. He was killed in a flying accident near Boisdinghem whilst taking part in a practice formation flight. His observer, Second Lieutenant Willie Jordan, was also killed in this accident. Both bodies were discovered with multiple injuries amongst the wreckage of Sopwith 7783. The two men share the same headstone in this cemetery, their inscriptions written one above the other. Lowe's inscription reads as follows: 'Second Lieutenant H.G.P. Lowe DCM Royal Flying Corps formerly Royal Engineers 8th November 1916 age 28. Glorious is the fruit of good labours.' Jordan's inscription reads: 'Second Lieutenant W. Jordan Royal Flying Corps 8th November 1916. Never forgotten.' Their shared grave reference number is IV.A.76.

TERLINCTHUN BRITISH CEMETERY

Major Arthur Willan Keen is buried in Terlincthun British Cemetery in Wimille, which is located on the northern outskirts of Boulogne. This cemetery contains 4,378 Commonwealth burials of the Great War. Joseph received instruction from Keen shortly after he joined the RFC and undertook four practice flights with him in November 1916. At this time Lieutenant Keen had one combat victory to his name, which he had scored whilst serving with No.70 Squadron. He later moved on to No.40 Squadron, where he scored a further 13 combat victories – firmly securing his status as an ace and bringing his final total to 14. He was awarded the Military Cross in August 1917 and his citation for this award reads as follows: 'For conspicuous gallantry and devotion to duty. He has shown the greatest gallantry and skill in aerial fighting, and his daring in leading offensive patrols into favourable positions for attack has been the means of many hostile aircraft being destroyed and driven down.' Keen was involved in a flying accident at Bruay Aerodrome on 15 August 1918, from which he suffered concussion and burns. He died of his injuries on 2 September 1918, aged 23. Keen's inscription reads: 'Major A.W. Keen, MC. Royal Air Force 2nd September 1918. Per ardua ad astra.' His grave reference is III.A.17.

Lowe's headstone at Longuenesse (Saint-Omer) Souvenir Cemetery (Lowe's image courtesy of Norfolk County Council Library and Information)

Keen's headstone at Terlincthun British Cemetery (Keen's image taken from Philip Lee Warner's Memorials of Rugbeians who fell in the Great War: Volume VI)

SECOND LIEUTENANT COCK

Second Lieutenant Geoffrey Hornblower Cock was Joseph's room-mate and the pair flew together on 13 separate occasions. On 22 July 1917, Cock took part in a photographic reconnaissance mission to Menin, flying with Lieutenant Maurice Moore as his observer. During this mission, their formation was attacked near Warneton by around 30 hostile aircraft. In the ensuing air combat a burst of enemy rounds put Cock's engine out of action and, to make matters worse, Moore's Lewis gun jammed after firing a single shot. It is a testament to Cock's skill as a pilot that he managed to land his damaged machine without being killed. He was, however, followed down by five enemy aircraft and taken prisoner of war along with Moore. During his time with the RFC, Cock was credited with shooting down at least 12 enemy aircraft, making him the highest-scoring ace to fly the Sopwith 1½ Strutter. He was awarded the Military Cross in June 1917 (gazetted in July) in recognition of his many achievements with No.45 Squadron, and his citation for this award reads as follows: 'For conspicuous gallantry and devotion to duty. On many occasions he showed great courage and determination in attacking and destroying hostile aircraft, and in dispersing hostile troops from a low altitude. His skill as a formation leader has set a fine example to the other pilots of his squadron.' Cock remained a prisoner of war until the war ended, finally returning to England on Christmas Day 1918. He went on to serve with the RAF during the Second World War, eventually retiring as a group captain in 1943. A truly remarkable character, he lived to the age of 84 and died in Belford, Northumberland, on 16 February 1980.

LIEUTENANT FRANCIS THOMAS COURTNEY

Lieutenant Francis Thomas Courtney was the OC 'B' Flight and flew with Joseph on one occasion – Boxing Day 1916, when they 'tested the weather' together. His stay at No.45 Squadron was, however, short-lived. Following an altercation with Brigadier Webb-Bowen, he was sent back to England. This altercation occurred shortly after the events of 6 April 1917, when No.45 Squadron lost six men over Tournai (see Tournai Communal Cemetery above). Courtney was not the only man within the squadron to feel 'sore' about these losses (see Joseph's Easter letter to his father, transcribed in chapter four), but he was perhaps the only man within the squadron brave enough to express his views openly to a superior officer. Many years later, Courtney wrote the following:

> Stories of my departure from No.45 went the rounds for a long time afterwards, with gleefully lurid versions of what I was supposed to have done or said to our Brigadier General… One day the Brigadier – who had never himself flown in any serious action – visited the squadron and broadcast some ill-timed comments that implied we were not using our planes to best effect. I replied with some undiluted remarks concerning the Brigade's directives. A few days later I was sent home.[52]

Once back in England, Courtney was made Fighting Instructor for the 18th Wing – a job he excelled at. After the war he relocated to America and enjoyed a highly successful career as a test pilot. A fearless and principled man, Courtney lived to the age of 88 and died in California in 1982.

LIEUTENANT ALEXANDER EVELYN CHARLWOOD

Lieutenant Alexander Evelyn Charlwood flew with Joseph on one occasion – a patrol over Steenwerke on 1 March 1917, during which they encountered one enemy aircraft. Charlwood was promoted to captain in July 1917 and posted to Home Establishment at the end of the following month. He was mentioned in despatches in 1919 for 'valuable services rendered during the Great War'. Charlwood lived to the age of 85 and died in Brighton in 1974.

Joseph acted as observer to a total of eight different pilots during his time with No.45 Squadron. Cock, Courtney and Charlwood were the only three to survive: Cock saved by being taken a prisoner of war, Courtney and Charlwood by being sent back to England prematurely.

SOPWITH A/8226

A replica Sopwith 1½ Strutter is currently (2019) on static display at the RAF Museum in Cosford, Shifnal, Shropshire TF11 8UP. This working replica was built by Viv Bellamy using original Sopwith factory drawings and was flown twice in September 1980. Not only is this a replica of the type of aircraft flown by Joseph's squadron, but it is also a replica of the actual aircraft in which

---

52 Frank T. Courtney, *Flight Path* (London: William Kimber & Co, 1973), p.105.

Joseph was mortally wounded on 9 May 1917 – bearing, as it does, the serial number A/8226. This particular aircraft started its operational career on 25 April 1917 and was used by 'C' Flight of No.45 Squadron. It ended its operational career on 27 May 1917, when it was shot down over enemy-held territory near Ypres with the loss of both Captain McArthur and Second Lieutenant Carey (see above). Second Lieutenant Cock had previously piloted A/8226 on 20 May 1917, on which date he shot down an Albatros scout near Lille.

Author standing next to replica Sopwith A/8226 at the RAF Museum in Cosford (photographed with the kind permission of the museum)

OTHER MEMORIALS

Joseph and Walter Senior are commemorated on the memorial plaques of St. Helen's Church in Sandal and St. John's Church in Wakefield, West Yorkshire. Their names also appear on the Wakefield (Queen Elizabeth) Grammar School War Memorial, along with all the other old boys who lost their lives in the Great War. This memorial was unveiled in 1921 and is located near the main entrance to the school, its location intended to remind future generations of the sacrifice of their predecessors. Each November the school holds a special service of remembrance around the war memorial, the most moving element of which is the playing of the last post by one of the current students.

The University of Cambridge has its own memorials and Joseph's name appears on two plaques here: one in the chapel of Clare College, and the other high on the right-hand side of the arched entrance to Memorial Court.

Both these plaques record all the fallen alumni of Clare College and included amongst their number is Joseph's school friend William Appleyard. Fellow RFC officers Francis George Truscott and Arthur Willan Keen were also alumni of the University of Cambridge and they are commemorated on oak panels in the chapel of Trinity College, a short walk away.

CHAPTER EIGHT
HULLABALOO

'Excusez-moi, Monsieur. Où est le cimetière?' I asked, holding up a photograph of my great-uncle.

The old man stooped towards my open car window and began to offer me directions in his native tongue.

'I'm sorry,' I interrupted, 'I don't speak French.'

This was not entirely true – as demonstrated by my initial question – but the reality was that my French vocabulary was limited. I could ask a simple question (with the aid of a dictionary), but was unable to understand the corresponding answer. Still, I had made an effort and had hoped that this would be sufficient for the old man to reply to me in English. Unfortunately this old man could no more speak my language than I could speak his. No matter. He promptly climbed into the passenger-side seat, pointed his index finger skywards and began to stir the air in a circular fashion. I made a 'U' turn and proceeded along the lane. Further hand gestures guided me right, and then right again, until I could see my destination up ahead. I stopped to let the old man out of the car, thanked him (in French), and then drove on a little further, watching in my wing mirror as he trudged back up the lane. Armed with cemetery plan and camera, I continued the last leg of my journey on foot, pausing before entry to take a photograph of the gateway to Bailleul Communal Cemetery. I later learnt that British soldiers, unsure how to pronounce the name of this town, had referred to it as 'Hullabaloo'. It seems I wasn't the first Englishman to struggle with the language.

It was late morning by the time I passed through the gateway and the spring sunshine was casting short, sharp shadows behind the ordered rows of gleaming headstones. What struck me most was how peaceful it all was. The grass was neatly cut and the flower beds along the rows were meticulously weed-free, like an idyllic country garden. Up ahead of me, I could see three people huddled in conversation at the end of one of the rows (as far as I can recall the only other people in the cemetery apart from me) and I instinctively made my way towards them. Although I had my cemetery plan to guide me, I felt a sudden need for company. I introduced myself and explained the reason for my visit, clumsily dropping my paperwork in the process. What followed next was an astonishing piece of good fortune: the trio included Gérard Lemaire (a leading member of a local history group) and Olivia D'Hau (a local tourism officer). Better still, all three could speak English. Gérard had been the driving force behind a book entitled 'Bailleul 1914-1918 British Garrison Town', which had been written by the local history society a few years earlier in order to commemorate the First World War. This book, which he was later kind enough to send me a copy of, included a paragraph about Joseph. After consulting my map, Gérard and Olivia pointed me in the right direction for row 'B' and held back whilst I walked on ahead to find my great-uncle.

Before I had set out that morning I had been quite excited at the prospect of visiting Joseph's grave, but now that I was finally here, standing before his headstone, I felt a sudden wave of emotion sweep over me – an overwhelming sense of sadness. I think it was his age that struck me most – 24 – exactly half my own. I took some photographs and was eventually joined by the others. Unexpectedly, Gérard then produced two poppies from his pocket and we placed one each upon the grave. I couldn't have planned a more appropriate way to commemorate the day. Before I left Bailleul I was treated to coffee in the centre and a tour of the town hall by Olivia – a firm reminder that the *entente cordiale* was still very much in evidence. Time, though, was ticking on and I still had one more cemetery to visit before the day's end.

The shadows were already starting to lengthen by the time I reached Thiepval and I had arrived far later than I had originally planned. I was also hungry. Rather like the man I was going to visit, I had 'not provided myself very liberally' and was in need of some sustenance. I found Connaught Cemetery easily enough, pleasantly situated in open countryside with the cool shelter of a wood behind. At Walter's grave I placed one of the poppies given to me by Gérard, and beside it a bluebell from my garden. I had brought two of these flowers with me from England, one for each of the brothers.

I knew very little about Walter when I first visited his grave. I wasn't even sure what he looked like. With Joseph there had been numerous condolence letters to gain an impression of the man, along with the smiling photograph of him in the rear cockpit of an aeroplane, but with Walter very little. Ironically, rather like the man himself, he was 'missing' to me. This was something I would rectify on my next trip, when I would return with a clearer mental image of who this man was. For now, though, I was drawn northwards towards the most prominent visible landmark – a tall monument which I later discovered to be the Ulster Tower. The adjacent shop was about to close up for the day, but I was just in time to buy a hot drink, which I enjoyed completely unaware that I was sitting within a stone's throw of 'The Triangle' – Walter's objective over a hundred years earlier.

I was tired by the time I returned to Talbot House. It was here, at Poperinge in Belgium, that I had booked a room the previous evening. Talbot House had been opened as an 'Every Man's Club' during the Great War. It was the brainchild of Army chaplains Philip 'Tubby' Clayton and Neville Talbot, who were looking to establish a peaceful environment for soldiers to come and forget the war between the fighting. 'Abandon rank all ye who enter here' was the only entry requirement – men and officers were to mix as equals. There was a piano for men to sing around; a garden where occasional concerts could be enjoyed; and an upstairs chapel high in the roof. There were also rooms available where men could read books or write letters. Nowadays it is run as a living museum, with bed and breakfast provided for those who wish to stay and soak up the atmosphere. Tubby's good humour still pervades the air and his witticisms appear on various signposts, e.g. 'Don't judge a man by his umbrella – It may not be his.'

On my final day I visited Ypres in order to witness the playing of the last post at the Menin Gate – a ceremony which takes place every evening here, without fail, at 8pm. I didn't need to ask for directions when I stepped off the bus. I simply followed the mass of people moving purposefully onwards. When the man in front of me learnt that this was my first visit, he gave up his place ahead of me in order that I should get a better view. The air of expectancy was tangible. Shortly before the bugler had even sounded his first note, an elderly woman to the right of me collapsed and had to be attended to by waiting paramedics. After the ceremony I took my time to read some of the names etched into the stone. The Menin Gate Memorial carries the names of more than 54,000 British and Commonwealth soldiers with no known graves who died defending the town. The undeniable poignancy of this statistic is counterbalanced by the enduring gratitude of the Belgian people here, which is evident from the smiles which appear whenever they hear a British accent.

Author besides Joseph's grave, photographed 9 May 2017

Author reading inscriptions at the Menin Gate Memorial, Ypres

It had been Martin Passande who suggested that I attend the Menin Gate ceremony. Martin was one of the wardens at Talbot House, and also a member of the Western Front Association. It was only later that I realised the particular significance of Ypres to my family history. Joseph had flown over the Ypres sector during his time with No.45 Squadron. Fellow airmen from his squadron had even crashed spectacularly into the town's moat during one of their patrols.[53] I had stared into the calm waters of this moat during my visit completely unaware of this fact. Had I known at the time, I might have been tempted to look skywards and imagine McArthur flying overhead with my great-uncle in the rear cockpit.

Being in France and Belgium gave me a much deeper understanding of the First World War. As soon as I returned to England I decided that my particular family history needed to be recorded properly. I had letters and a photograph album to help my research. I had even been fortunate enough to make contact with Gérard, who was able to provide me with detailed local knowledge of Bailleul – knowledge which, amongst other things, enabled me to identify the location of Casualty Clearing Station No.53. Perhaps most significant of all, though, was Martin's suggestion that I pay a visit to the National Archives in London. I visited here the following month, having preordered War Office files relating to Joseph, Walter and George. The very survival of these files was a minor miracle in itself, as many Army records had been destroyed by fire during the Second World War. Some of the pages relating to Walter even bore scorch marks around their edges as if to testify to this fact.[54] The records themselves made fascinating reading, but were often incomplete or difficult to decipher. Scratching beneath the surface often led to unexpected revelations, as was the

---

53 No.45 Squadron lost two machines over Ypres on 11 March 1917 with the loss of all four airmen: Captain Lubbock and Lieutenant Thompson, flying in A/1082; and Second Lieutenant Bowden and Second Lieutenant Stevenson, flying in A/1071. The squadron record book records that A/1082 'fell in moat at Ypres', and that A/1071 'fell 28 I 9 b'. A later hand has amended this entry in pencil to indicate that it was in fact A/1071 that landed in the moat (TNA AIR 1/1787/204/151/4).

54 I had less luck when contacting the federal archives of Germany via the *bundesarchiv.de* website. I had written (in my best German) to request copies of the combat reports for Jasta 28 on 9 May 1917. In reply to my email, I was regrettably informed that no combat reports for this German fighter squadron had survived to the present day: The records of the Prussian Army were, for the most part, destroyed by the fire at the military archives which was caused by an air raid on Potsdam in 1945. The irony was not lost on me.

case when I asked my optician for help in assessing Walter's acuteness of vision as recorded on his Army medical certificate. In the course of his explanation, Mr Bamrah revealed that his grandfather had fought for the British in one of the many Sikh regiments. There were few people I spoke to who did not have some connection to this monumental conflict.

One trip to the National Archives proved to be insufficient. Names which were thrown up by my initial visit were clearly in need of further research – in particular Captain Hearn and Second Lieutenant Mitchell. The squadron records also needed examination and these, in turn, threw up yet more names. Frustratingly, I was unable to find where on the battlefield Walter's body was originally found. This elusive grid reference would perhaps have solved the mystery of how he had died. Despite this disappointment, I found far more information than I could reasonably have expected. I also uncovered many surprising facts: an accounts form revealed that Joseph had been paid in advance for the month of May, and since he had not served for the whole of this month (due to his death on the 9th) 22 days' pay would now have to be deducted from his final pay packet. The overpayment amounted to 13 pounds and four shillings. From this it is possible to work out that Joseph's salary as an RFC officer amounted to 12 shillings a day.[55] Another surprise was the record which listed the full inventory of items which were in Joseph's possession at the time of his death:

> 1 Advance Book *6946*; 2 Book Cheque Counterfoils; 1 Cheque Book; 1 Tobacco Pouch; 2 Pipes & 4 Tubes; 1 Cigarette Case; 1 Holy Bible; 1 Pocket Chess; 1 Silk Scarf; 1 Handkerchief; 1 Collar; 1 Tie; 1 pair Goggles (aviation) *damaged*; 1 Penknife; 1 Watch; 1 Note Case; 1 Wallet with photographic negatives; 1 Photo Case & photos; 2 Notebooks; 1 Diary; 1 Calendar; Photos, private papers, letters, etc; 2 Magazines; 1 Cigarette Tube in case; 1 Whistle & cord; 1 Set Regtl Buttons; 4 Coat Badges, West Yorks Rgt; 4

---

55 This accounts form, dated 7 February 1918, is to be found within TNA WO 339/1739. In the days of pre-decimalised currency there were 12 pence in a shilling and 20 shillings in a pound. There are online tools which can convert old money into their equivalent worth today to give some sense of their relative buying power.

Embroidered Stars; 1 Observers Brevet; 1 Monocle; 1 Yale Key; 1
Spanner; 1 Collar Stud; 1 Wrist Watch; 1 Fountain Pen, broken; 1
Tie Pin; 1 pkt Lamels; 1 Cheque No. RFC/X049863, dated 19-11-
16 for ½d. drawn on Messrs Cox & Co, by 2nd Lt. P.H. Tod, R.F.C.
in favour of J.T. Senior, and crossed.[56]

Standing out amongst this list of items are the damaged aviation goggles, presumably damaged in Joseph's final flight. The pocket chess set is of further interest as Joseph's brother George was also a chess player. My father gave me Grandpa George's pocket chess set when I was a boy, telling me that George had it with him during the war. Made from leather and the size of a small notebook, the chessboard has slits for the ivorine chess markers to slot into. Once folded, the board fits snugly into its dark green cover. Joseph's chess set may well have been similar in design. It is even possible that they are one and the same, i.e. the set may have been passed on to George following Joseph's death.

Amongst its other items, the inventory also mentions a watch and a wristwatch. No wristwatch has been passed on down through the family, but a watch has. This watch, engraved with Joseph's initials, appears to have been given to him as a 21st birthday present and would have been one of his most prized possessions. Other than that, the photo case is the only other definite survivor. What happened to Joseph's diary is a mystery. Another mystery concerns the final item on the list – a cheque for the derisory sum of half a penny. The date of the cheque reveals that it had been written out in Joseph's favour almost six months earlier when No.45 Squadron was based at Boisdinghem. The writer of the cheque, Second Lieutenant P.H. Tod, does not, however, appear to have served with No.45 Squadron and it therefore follows that he was attached to another squadron based on the same aerodrome or else one nearby. The only rational explanation for this cheque is that it was written as part of a private joke between the two men.[57]

---

56 This inventory, dated 19 May 1917, is to be found within TNA WO 339/1739.

57 There is a record of a Lieutenant P.H. Tod to be found on the Forces War Records website and it records
that he served with the Canadian Army Service Corps. It is just possible that Joseph had given Tod a
halfpenny stamp for a letter, with the cheque being reimbursement.

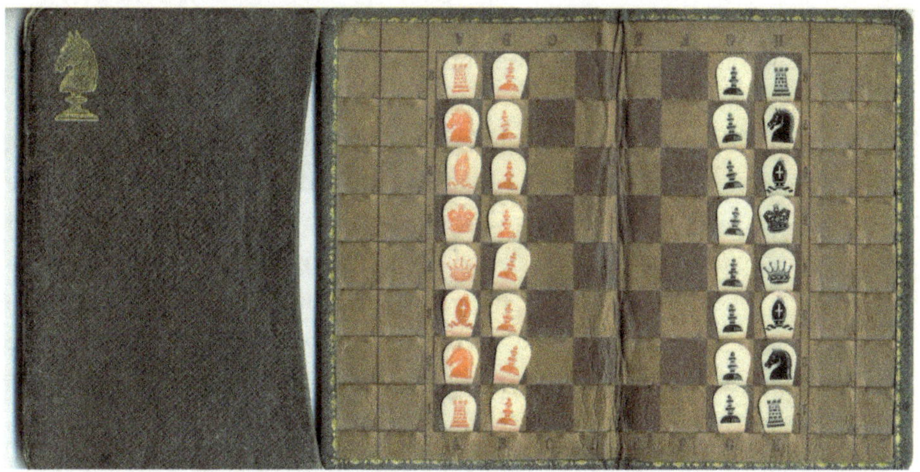

George's pocket chess set, played on during the war (Author's collection)

Joseph's watch, engraved with his monogrammed initials on the reverse side. The surviving warranty indicates that it was purchased on 13 May 1913 – nine days before Joseph's 21st birthday. The makers' name is clearly visible on the face of the watch: Kendal & Dent were based at 106 Cheapside, London, E.C. and were 'chronometer makers to the Admiralty'.

(Author's collection)

Once I had collated information from the National Archives, I was able to piece together a chronology from enlistment onwards. Amongst my grandfather's effects (which had been passed on to me via my father) I found further letters, postcards and cuttings. These all helped me to continue and expand the process. I also came across George's KOYLI jacket and Walter's school cap, his name written on the inner lining. Perhaps the most exciting resource at my disposal was Joseph's photograph album, which I had discovered before my first trip to Bailleul. None of the photographs in this album were labelled, and prior to my trip I had only been able to positively identify one picture of Joseph – the only one in his album which had been duplicated and blown up. Paradoxically, it was a picture in which his face was almost completely obscured by an aviation mask – which is how I knew it must be him. Any lingering doubt that it truly was Joseph was removed when I found corroborating evidence a year later through Colin Huston of Cross & Cockade International. Colin's help also enabled me to identify many other photographs from the latter pages of Joseph's album.

Here credit must also go to retired Wing Commander C.G. Jefford for his excellent history of No.45 Squadron. It was Jeff's book which led me to the photograph of Joseph standing next to Sopwith A/8226. Other photographic help came from correspondence with relatives of the dead airmen – namely Maggie Strutt (relative of H.G.P. Lowe's) and Nick Blake (great-nephew of J.E. Blake). Blake's likeness proved to be the most difficult to verify, but a group family photograph proved extremely helpful in this respect.

Good fortune played a hand in many areas of my research. A timely email to Wakefield (Queen Elizabeth) Grammar School led to the discovery that the school was soon to publish a book detailing all the old boys who had fought in the Great War. The title of this book ('Some Other and Wider Destiny') even took its inspiration from ex-headmaster Joseph Barton's condolence letter to Arthur following Joseph's death.[58] The book had been co-written by Elaine Merckx (school archivist) and Neal Rigby (retired Head of History) and both were extremely helpful in providing me with information on the brothers' schooldays. Their book also led to the discovery of four additional letters written by Joseph to school friend Stanley Dixon (which had been

---

58 Mr Barton's condolence letter is quoted in full towards the end of chapter four.

preserved by Stanley's grandson, Philip Dixon). This knowledge enabled me to positively identify the 'Stanley' who had previously written several postcards to Joseph.

Walter's school cap (Author's collection)

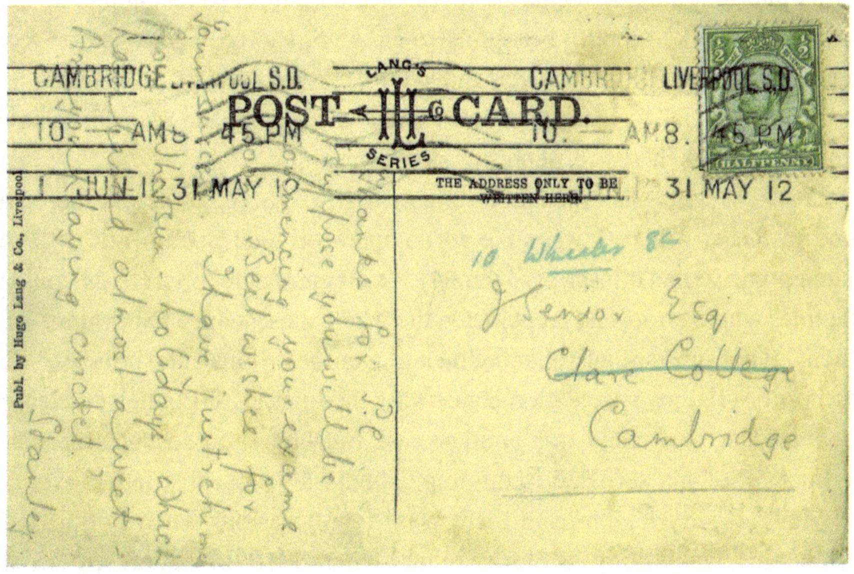

Stanley Dixon's postcard to Joseph, written 31 May 1912 (Author's collection)

I took care to accurately transcribe all the documents in my possession, but an early mistake occurred when I wrongly transcribed the letter 'c' as the letter 'o'. The consequence of this error was that I initially believed that one of Joseph's condolence letters had been sent by a G.H. Cook (as opposed to G.H. Cock). My mistake was perhaps excusable – the same mistake had been made by the *Wakefield Express* on 19 May 1917, when it reproduced an extract from Cock's condolence letter and wrongly referred to him as 'pilot G.H. Cook'. The reason for our shared mistake eventually became clear: unlike the other letters in my possession, the condolence letters were not the originals. They were contemporary typed copies of the originals and the lower-case letters 'c' and 'o' were almost indistinguishable due to the particular font of the typewriter. It seems that Arthur arranged for several typed copies to be made soon after Joseph's death in order that these could be shared with other family members. It also seems as though he made one set of copies available to the *Wakefield Express* in order to provide them with information for their article on Joseph. I had been 'reading from the same book' as the *Wakefield Express* and we had both seen the wrong letter within the letter. The eventual realisation of my mistake came to light whilst leafing through the pages of Trevor Henshaw's seminal work 'The Sky Their Battlefield', a book which 'provides a definitive detailed listing and description of over four years of continuous fighting in the air in WW1'. Here I happened to stumble upon the name 'G.H. Cock' – a pilot belonging to No.45 Squadron. The squadron record book later confirmed that this was indeed the correct spelling. That single letter 'c' became crucial to locating Cock's archival records, and also to positively identifying his likeness in Joseph's photograph album.

Cross-checking documents became central to my research and there were some instances where I was able to compare original documents with their contemporary typed transcripts – namely the air combat reports. Here I could see examples where errors had crept in. On the whole these tended to be minor errors which did not substantially alter the meaning of the original. Nevertheless, these observations fed my speculation concerning the final 'e' of Lieutenant Hearne's surname. Doctor Greene was another case in point – on Joseph's headstone the final 'e' of his surname is missing. Thankfully, Joseph's letters were, on the whole, clearly legible, and there were few occasions when I struggled to decipher his handwriting. Walter's solitary letter did, however, present me with one word over which I laboured for some considerable time: 'enriched'.

27 Earls' Avenue
Folkestone
4 March 1915

Dear Bessie

I am sending you one of our Regimental brooches, which I got in Folkestone the other night: hope you will like it. We arrived here all safe last Monday feeling very fit. The weather was remarkably good the whole time & my face is quite red now with the sun. Most of the men stuck it very well indeed: we covered 117 miles in the 7 days & had comparatively few men falling out. One day we did 25 miles or more, Dorking to Edenbridge, but got into the latter place almost at our last gasp. My feet were rather weary & I developed a small blister, but was really troubled very little on the whole. Kitchener inspected us on the Sunday: we marched past him on the road. I was the first platoon in my company & gave him 'eyes right' with great gusto. He was very pleased with our appearance & is reported to have said 'The First Army is good, the Second is better, but the Third (ours) licks them all', so we feel quite happy. Folkestone is swarming with French & Belgian people, many of them wounded soldiers, who are convalescing here. Our men are all put up in Boarding Houses, where they have everything provided by the people of the house, bed, food. etc.; & as they have been previously accustomed to Army rations only, seem to be living in comparative luxury. We Officers, I think, are faring worst of all: we are put into an empty house, which we have to furnish ourselves, if we want furniture, & have to sleep in our camp-beds, which after all are nothing like so comfortable as a spring mattress etc. We were put into private

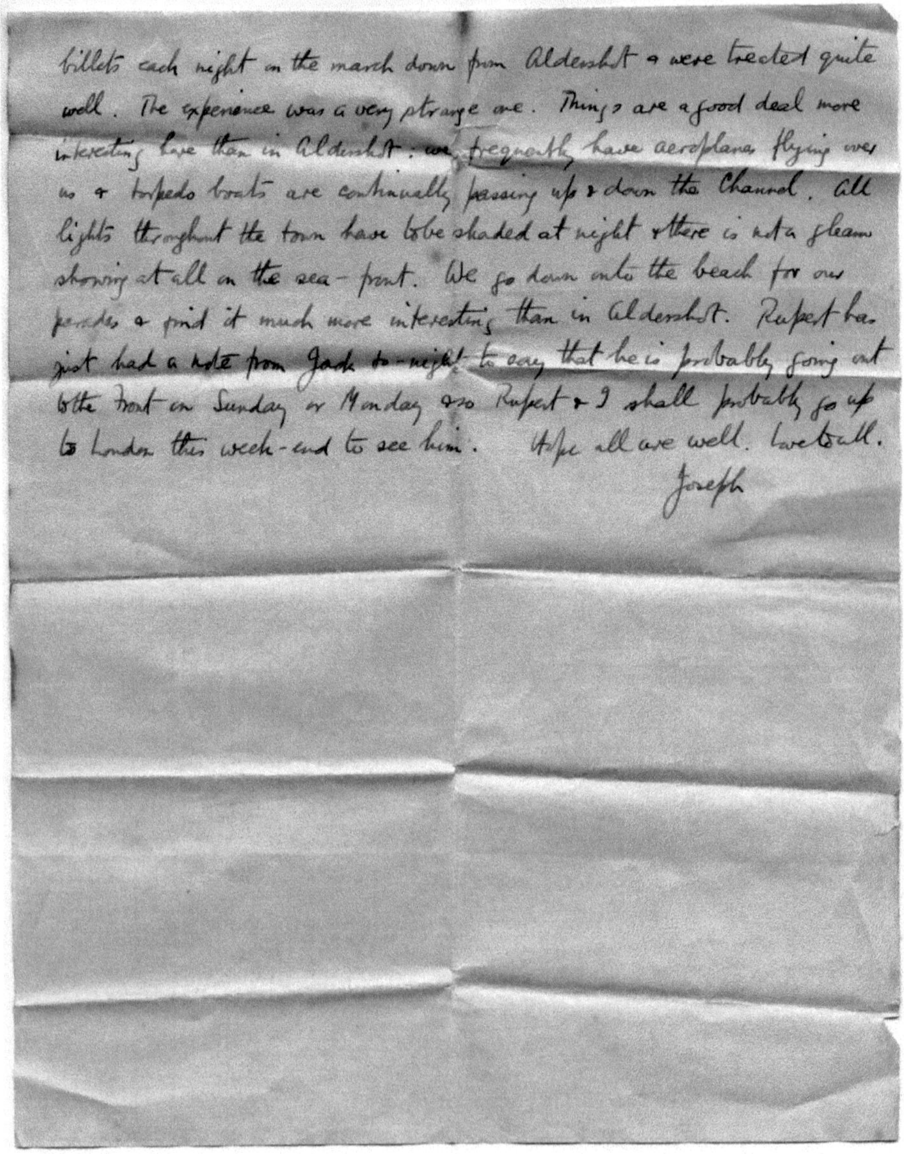

billets each night on the march down from Aldershot & were treated quite well. The experience was a very strange one. Things are a good deal more interesting here than in Aldershot: we frequently have aeroplanes flying over us & torpedo boats are continually passing up & down the Channel. All lights throughout the town have to be shaded at night & there is not a gleam showing at all on the sea-front. We go down onto the beach for our parades & find it much more interesting than in Aldershot. Rupert has just had a note from Jack to-night to say that he is probably going out to the front on Sunday or Monday & so Rupert & I shall probably go up to London this week-end to see him. Hope all are well. Love to all.

Joseph

Joseph's letter to Bessie, written 4 March 1915 (Author's collection)

I returned to France in May 2018, a year after my initial trip. This time my starting point was Thiepval, where I began by revisiting Walter's grave. I then paid my respects to 'The Professor' – Second Lieutenant Charles Henry Mitchell – buried at Mill Road Cemetery nearby. I had come to Thiepval with a specific goal in mind: I wanted to discover the last known location of these two men. Prior to my trip, I had consulted a historic trench map of the area (Beaumont 57D.S.E.1. & 2.) and overlaid it onto a modern satellite image. By lining up the two images, using Thiepval Wood as a useful reference point, I was able to gain a rough approximation of where I should look. It appeared from the combined images that 'The Sunken Road' followed the same course as part of the modern tarmacked road (the D73) and I could see that this section ran close to the Ulster Tower. I asked the custodian of the tower if he could confirm its location for me and it transpired that there was more than one 'sunken road' in the area (the other one being at Beaumont-Hamel), but the one near the tower was indeed the one I was looking for. The man also pointed me in the direction of the observation post at 'The Pope's Nose'. I walked along the rough track between the arable fields until I reached the twisted metal poking out of the ground. I knew I must be standing close to point 16 of 'The Triangle'. Turning back to face Thiepval Wood, I imagined what it must have been like for Walter all those years ago. In which direction would *I* have run? What thoughts would have been rushing through my mind as I picked my way back across no man's land?

Before leaving the area, I returned to the Ulster Tower to fill up my water bottle. As I did so, I noticed various rusting artillery shell casings piled up in a corner. Next to them was a bucket filled with lead shot. These smooth grey balls of metal, half an inch in diameter, had been taken from an unexploded shrapnel shell which had been discovered in an adjoining field. Even 100 years after the conflict, such discoveries are apparently a common occurrence here. I held some of this shrapnel in the palm of my hand and rolled it slowly between my fingers. It still amazes me that I was able to touch an artefact linked so closely to my great-uncle.

The Thiepval Memorial was a short drive away. Here I paid my respects to Lieutenant Turner, Lance Corporal Pearce and Second Lieutenant Bottomley. I could hear the hollow drumming of great spotted woodpeckers in the avenue of trees as I approached. It seemed to mimic the gentle echo of machine-gun fire from a different era. An assistant helped me to locate the names I was looking for and I craned my neck to take the relevant photos. As I was leaving, I noticed a party of school children that had just arrived. The children sat excitedly on the grass while their teacher explained something to them in a language I was too far away to hear. There were intermittent whooping sounds from the young students and then they were unleashed on the monument. They ran laughing and smiling and pointing at the countless names. It seemed more like a treasure hunt than an educational visit. I wondered what the dead soldiers would have made of the spectacle.

As I approached Harelbeke in Belgium the following morning, I could see the vapour trails of half a dozen aeroplanes criss-crossing the horizon. Strange names on passing signposts pointed to places I had previously seen only on the pages of the No.45 Squadron Record Book. Dixmude, Roubaix, Courtrai – all these names were thrown into immediate context by my journey. As I drove, it occurred to me that I was travelling on land at a speed not dissimilar to that of a Sopwith 1½ Strutter in the air. I had the disembodied voice of sat nav for company. One hundred years ago the voice might have been that of an observer communicating with his pilot through a crude rubber speaking tube. The pilot I was visiting today was someone I felt I knew well and someone I had so wanted to have lived beyond the war. Alas, no. Like so many airmen who served with the Royal Flying Corps, it was not so much a matter of whether or not you died as when. The visit to McArthur's final resting place was as moving as I had expected. Before I left Harlebeke New British Cemetery I placed flowers before both his and Carey's headstone. Then I continued towards Tournai.

I felt uneasy about waking the man, but there was nobody else to ask and I wasn't even sure if I was at the right place. Despite the initial protest that he was on his break, the groundskeeper (if that is what he was) took me to the relevant section of the enormous communal cemetery. I suspect that if I had not been English, he would have told me to sling my hook. Bleary-eyed, he returned to the seat of his parked car and I pressed on to find the six airmen of No.45 Squadron who had all been shot down on the same day in 'Bloody April'. Amongst their number was Truscott, the son of a London Lord Mayor and a close friend of Joseph's. The bottom line of Truscott's epitaph was completely obscured by dirt. I gently brushed with my hand until the line was revealed. Then I smiled – 'God is here' – it seemed an appropriate place to find Him.

My visit to Bailleul Communal Cemetery was timed to coincide with the anniversary of Joseph's death (as it had been the previous year) and I arrived here at 9:30 a.m. on the Wednesday. Soon to join me were Jérôme Grosse and Olivia D'Hau, in a meeting arranged by Gérard Lemaire. Jérôme was an expert in the field of aviation and author of *'Terrains d'aviation militaires Première*

Guerre mondiale'. He was here to drive me to the location of No.45 Squadron aerodrome at Sainte-Marie-Cappel. Before we set off he gave me a copy of his book as a gift and I, in turn, gave him a copy of Norman Macmillan's book 'Into the Blue'. We then took a short detour to see a ploughed field. The churned soil had been the location of No.1 Squadron aerodrome. It was here that McArthur had touched down in order for Joseph to receive medical treatment for his gunshot wounds. Next we drove past the new mental health centre which stands on the site of the old asylum – where Joseph had died.

In the blink of an eye we were standing next to an old farmhouse and I was looking (optimistically) for a pond. We had arrived at our destination. Without Jérôme's help, I would never have been able to find the location of No.45 Squadron aerodrome and now that we were here I had a chance to literally walk in the footsteps of my great-uncle. It seemed an idyllic spot to have an airfield with its flat terrain and picturesque countryside all around. On the northern horizon I could see Mont Cassel and immediately understood its significance as a navigation aid for the airmen. As it gradually came into view, it must have been a reassuring beacon for returning patrols. Unsurprisingly there was no trace of the Nissen huts which had served as the men's sleeping quarters all those years ago. Young poplar trees were, however, to be found beyond the large field adjoining the farm. These were possible descendants of the ones which had surrounded the tented area used later by the men. As for my pond – I did find one, but whether or not it was the one used by the squadron for firing practice is highly questionable. I would not therefore be returning home with spent shells from the silt.

Before we left the area, we drove into the village of Sainte-Marie-Cappel. Here Jérôme managed to track down Patrice Deneux, who was the local history expert. We sat in his conservatory and discussed the aerodrome whilst Madame Deneux poured cups of tea (with milk for the Englishman). It had been a truly memorable day. I was dropped back at Bailleul Cemetery shortly after 6 p.m. The significance of the hour dawned on me a little later as I sat alone on a stone bench overlooking the graveyard.

The *Notre-Dame de la Crypte* church at Cassel was the last place I visited on the final day of my trip. I have no solid evidence that Joseph ever visited this church, but my instincts tell me that he did. If my instincts are correct, then he may well have noticed his name etched in stone on the right as you enter. There are in fact dedications to two Josephs here – Josephus Antonius and Josephus Benedictus – as a classical scholar, Joseph would have enjoyed the challenge of translating their Latin inscriptions. Also to be found in this church is a statue of the Madonna with Child, situated above a side altar. Joseph's own mother had died when he was nine and if he did ever visit this church, he may well have been drawn to this image. One man who certainly did visit the *Notre-Dame de la Crypte* was Marshal Ferdinand Foch, who is known to have prayed here during one of several visits to the town. His bronzed image adorns one of the central columns within the church. Outside there is a memorial to the young men of Cassel who died for France during the years 1914-1918. I paused here to reflect before driving on to Calais, my route back to England.

The Great War has now passed out of living memory. That is why it is so important to record in print the deeds of the men who fought and were killed. This has been my attempt. I can think of no better way to end this book than by adapting the words which appear on the memorial scrolls sent by the War Office to Arthur Senior in memory of his two lost sons, Joseph and Walter:

Those whom this book commemorates were numbered among those who, at the call of King and Country, left all that was dear to them, endured hardness, faced danger, and finally passed out of the sight of men by the path of duty and self-sacrifice, giving up their own lives that others might live in freedom. Let those who come after see to it that their names be not forgotten.

Acknowledgements

I wish to acknowledge the help and advice given to me by the following individuals: Neal Rigby, Elaine Merckx (Queen Elizabeth Grammar School, Wakefield); Philip Dixon (grandson of Robert Stanley Dixon); Matthew Thomas (Wakefield Library); Gérard Lemaire (*Cercle d'histoire et d'archéologie de Bailleul Monts de Flandre*), Olivia D'Hau (*Référent Tourisme et Relations internationales*), Jérôme Grosse (*Membre d'Anciens Aérodromes*), Patrice Deneux (Sainte-Marie-Cappel aviation expert); Colin Huston (Cross & Cockade International); C.G. Jefford MBE (retired RAF Wing Commander); Dr R.J.E. Thompson, Jude Brimmer (University of Cambridge); Oliver Wilkinson (University of Wolverhampton); Rob Gray (Head of Research, Royal Signals Museum, Blandford Camp); Russ Gannon (The Aerodrome); Martin Passande, John Gilder (Western Front Association); Martin Skelly (CWGC Records Department); Maggie Strutt (relative of H.G.P. Lowe's); Nick Blake (great-nephew of J.E. Blake); Anne Bradley (Bristol Grammar School archivist); Joyce Millar (Harvington School secretary); Narinder Bamrah (optometrist); Zahid Al-Gafoor (director of 'Image Centre'); Henry & Miriam Gent, Jill Crisp, Guy Talbot (relatives).

Archival Records

The National Archives, Kew, Richmond, Surrey:
TNA AIR 1/1786/204/151/1 (45 Squadron Combat Reports 01/10/16–30/11/18)
TNA AIR 1/1787/204/151/3 (45 Squadron Record Book 01/10/16–31/12/16)
TNA AIR 1/1787/204/151/4 (45 Squadron Record Book 01/01/17–30/06/17)
TNA AIR 76/84/143 (A.E. Charlwood)
TNA AIR 76/108/13 (F.T. Courtney)
TNA AIR 76/269/150 (A.W. Keen)
TNA AIR 76/312/42 (L.W. McArthur)
TNA AIR 76/550/20 (W.G.B. Williams)
TNA FO 383/506 (Germany: Prisoners, including: Correspondence on the submission of reports relating to prisoner of war camps)
TNA MH 106/497 (S.G. Hearn)
TNA WO 95/3025/4 (2/6 Battalion Sherwood Foresters; Nottingham & Derbyshire Regiment)
TNA WO 339/1739 (J. Senior)
TNA WO 339/22819 (D.W. Edwards)
TNA WO 339/61967 (G.H. Cock)
TNA WO 339/59987 (J.E. Blake)
TNA WO 374/8721 (W.S. Brayshay)
TNA WO 374/32310 (S.G. Hearn)
TNA WO 374/43517 (L.W. McArthur)
TNA WO 374/48096 (C.H. Mitchell)
TNA WO 374/61329 (G. Senior)
TNA WO 374/61338 (W.T. Senior)
TNA WO 374/69849 (E.A. Turner)

KING'S COLLEGE ARCHIVE CENTRE OF THE UNIVERSITY OF CAMBRIDGE:

AEF/4/11 (German prisoners of war held at Blandford Camp in 1917)

GERMAN RECORDS:

Nachrichtenblatt der Luftstreitkräfte (intelligence report of the German Air Force)

Kommandeur der Flieger 4 Armee (Air Commander report of the German 4 Army on the Ypres sector)

SELECTED BIBLIOGRAPHY

Mike O'Connor, *Airfields & Airmen Ypres* (Great Britain: Pen & Sword Books, 2014; first published by Leo Cooper, 2001)

Frank T. Courtney, *Flight Path* (London: William Kimber & Co, 1973)

Philippe Ducrocq, *Bailleul 1914–1918 British Garrison Town* (France: Cercle d'histoire et d'archéologie de Bailleul Monts de Flandre, 2014)

Margaret Franklin, *Harvington School for Girls, Ealing: A History on the Occasion of the Centenary 1890-1990* (Ealing: M. Franklin, 1990)

Norman Franks, Frank Bailey and Rick Duiven, *The Jasta War Chronology: A Complete Listing of Claims and Losses, August 1916 – November 1918* (London: Grub Street, 1998)

Robert Graves, *Goodbye to All That* (London: Penguin Books, 1960; first published by Jonathan Cape, 1929)

Trevor Henshaw, *The Sky Their Battlefield* (London: Grub Street, 1995)

C.G. Jefford MBE BA RAF Retd, *The Flying Camels: The History of No 45 Sqn, RAF* (Great Britain: C.G. Jefford, 1995)

Cecil Lewis, *Sagittarius Rising* (London: Peter Davies, 1936)

Norman Macmillan OBE MC AFC, *Into the Blue* (London: Grub Street, 2015; first published by Gerald Duckworth & Co, 1929)

Graham Mark, *Prisoners of war in British hands during WW1: a study of their history, the camps and their mails* (Great Britain: The Postal History Society, 2007)

Elaine Merckx & Neal Rigby, *Some Other and Wider Destiny: Wakefield Grammar School Foundation and the Great War* (Solihull: Helion & Company, 2017)

Sue Ryder, *And the Morrow Is Theirs* (Bristol: Sue Ryder Foundation, 1975)

R.B. Sayce, *A Rural Surveyor* (Wantage: R.B. Sayce, 2000)

Jack Sheldon, *The Germans At Thiepval* (Great Britain: Pen & Sword Books, 2006)

Captain E.V. Tempest DSO MC, *History of the Sixth Battalion West Yorkshire Regiment: Volume 1-1/6th Battalion* (Bradford: Percy Lund, Humphries & Co, 1921)

Philip Lee Warner, *Memorials of Rugbeians who fell in the Great War: Volumes IV & VI* (Rugby: The Medici Society, 1918 & 1921)

WEBSITES

The Aerodrome
Ancestry
Commonwealth War Graves Commission
Cross & Cockade International
Forces War Records
General Register Office (birth, death and marriage certificates)
The Great War Forum
Imperial War Museum

INDEX

Note: an 'n' after a page number indicates that the reference is contained in the footnote(s).